PRAYING
TOGETHER

PRAYING TOGETHER

Forming Prayer Ministries
in
Your Congregation

MARTHA GRAYBEAL ROWLETT

UPPER
ROOM BOOKS®
NASHVILLE

PRAYING TOGETHER
FORMING PRAYER MINISTRIES IN YOUR CONGREGATION
Copyright © 2002 by Martha Graybeal Rowlett
All rights reserved.

The Upper Room® Web site: http://www.upperroom.org.

Scripture quotations are from the New Revised Standard Version Bible, copyright 1989, Division of Christian Education of the National Council of the Churches of Christ in the United States of America. Used by permission. All rights reserved.

The publisher gratefully acknowledges the following copyright holders for permission to use copyrighted material:

Excerpts from *Covenant Discipleship* by David Lowes Watson (Nashville, Tenn.: Discipleship Resources, 1991) and *Forming Christian Disciples* by David Lowes Watson (Nashville, Tenn.: Discipleship Resources, 1995). Used by permission of the author.

"Guidelines for Centering Prayer" from *The Method of Centering Prayer* by Thomas Keating. Copyright © 1995 St. Benedict's Monastery. Used by permission of Contemplative Outreach, Ltd.

Excerpts from *Spiritual Life in the Congregation.* Copyright © 1997 by Rueben P. Job. Used by permission of Upper Room Books.

Excerpts from *An Adventure in Healing and Wholeness* by James K. Wagner. Copyright © 1993 by The Upper Room. Used by permission of Upper Room Books.

Cover and interior design: Thelma Whitworth
Cover photograph: SuperStock
Interior implementation: PerfecType, Nashville, Tennessee
First printing: 2002

Library of Congress Cataloging-in-Publication Data
Rowlett, Martha Graybeal.
    Praying together : forming prayer ministries in your congregation / by Martha Graybeal Rowlett.
    p. cm.
Includes bibliographical references.
    ISBN 0-8358-0979-X
    1. Prayer—Christianity.   I. Title.
BV210.3 .R69 2002
248.3'2—dc21   2002002489

Printed in the United States of America

Contents

Preface

In recent years, local churches have offered a wide range of opportunities for Christians to pray with one another. A bountiful smorgasbord of possibilities for prayer ministries and a constantly expanding set of resources are currently available. This book provides a summary of some of these contemporary prayer ministries in an attempt to help churches sort out the options and choose those models best suited to their needs.

Contributions to this book have come from many sources. The initial idea for a book like this came from Janice Grana, former book editor for The Upper Room. Her professional guidance and encouragement have been invaluable. Helpful support for its development has come from The Upper Room staff members who have provided consultation and materials. Cherie Jones convened a staff consultation to launch the project. Stephen Bryant, publisher of The Upper Room, has offered a basic vision of prayer as a lifestyle for a local congregation rather than a specialized ministry among other ministries. This book is intended to serve that vision.

Special thanks go to the more than 150 people who responded to my request for local church examples of people praying together. Beth Richardson e-mailed my invitation to The Upper Room leadership list, and e-mails, letters, and telephone calls flooded back to my desk from across the nation and around the world. Reporting churches are widely scattered geographically. Large churches and small churches, city churches and rural churches, laypeople and clergy generously shared wisdom and insight, words of encouragement, offers of prayer, helpful information, and inspiring stories. These responses have given both shape and content to this book. The names of those whose stories, models, or Voices of Experience are included in this book are acknowledged here, and, where they have given permission, their names are used in the text with their contributions.

Susan Peek of United Methodist Communications conducted a similar poll to assist with the chapter on Internet prayer ministry, and her assistance was productive in terms of both local-church and denominational resources. Other major sources include:

- books recommended by consultants who served on this project;

- portrayals of people praying together from scripture;

- experiences with prayer ministries from my own life and ministry as a pastor in local churches.

A book like this could become a catalog of products with a promotional pitch for each. I hope this book avoids that danger. You will find here descriptions of a range of options for local-church prayer ministries. I hope that you also will find here inspiration in the stories shared by those who have found faith and hope and love in the process of praying together with other Christians. May this book contribute to the presence of a praying church of Jesus Christ in the twenty-first century!

Acknowledgments

The following persons contributed stories, descriptions, models, and Voices of Experience for prayer ministries in congregations that are included in this book. (Names are listed in alphabetical order.) An asterisk by a name indicates that more than one contribution from that person is included. A special note of thanks is due to Priscilla Van Giesen of the United Methodist Church of the Resurrection in Leawood, Kansas, who could have written this book from her experience as director of prayer ministries for her church if she had not been so busy making possible all that she has shared here. More than one hundred additional contributions arrived in response to an invitation to the e-mail leadership list of The Upper Room. Space limitations prevent the use of all of them. They provided perspective and inspiration for the task of writing this book. Thanks be to God for those who pray with others and are willing to share that experience.

Pam Abbey, Concord United Methodist Church, Concord, California; **Carla Badgett**, St. Luke's United Methodist Church, Houston, Texas; **Ann Barry**, First Parish Church,

United Church of Christ, Brunswick, Maine; **Lore Baymor**, First Presbyterian Church, Stroudsburg, Pennsylvania; **Maxine Bolden**, Anderson United Methodist Church, Jackson, Mississippi; **Fran Boyer**, Hudson United Methodist Church, Hudson, Ohio; **Ken Carter**, Mount Tabor United Methodist Church, Winston-Salem, North Carolina; **Melody Christolear**, First United Methodist Church, Tuscaloosa, Alabama; **John Clifford**, First United Methodist Church, Comanche, Texas; **Kathy Crane**,* First Presbyterian Church, Stroudsburg, Pennsylvania; **Bruce and Teresa Erickson**, Life Bible Fellowship, Upland, California; **Fran Fletcher**, Gulf Breeze United Methodist Church, Gulf Breeze, Florida; **David W. Gould III**, Bon Air United Methodist Church, Richmond, Virginia; **Kathy Grecco**, Sterling United Methodist Church, Sterling, Pennsylvania; **Susan Gregg-Schroeder**, First United Methodist Church, San Diego, California; **Pat Griffith**, Lake Cities United Methodist Church, Lake Dallas, Texas; **Delia Halverson**, Faith Discovery Ministries, Ft. Myers, Florida; **Priscilla Hanford**, Paradise United Methodist Church, Paradise, California; **Sheryl Hartley**, United Methodist Church of the Resurrection, Leawood, Kansas; **Dee Hazen**,* San Clemente Presbyterian Church, San Clemente, California; **Ron Hopperton**,

12

First United Methodist Church, Orange, Texas; **Anne Hornkohl**, First Presbyterian Church, Stroudsburg, Pennsylvania; **Shirley Hutchison**, South Street Christian Church (Disciples of Christ), Springfield, Missouri; **Todd C. Karges**, First United Methodist Church, Lexington, Nebraska; **Mary Liz Kehoe**, Bon Air United Methodist Church, Richmond, Virginia; **Linelle Kelley**, Inman United Methodist Church, Inman, Nebraska; **Joyce Leach**, Nestor United Methodist Church, San Diego, California; **Nancy LeValley**, Asbury United Methodist Church, Traverse City, Michigan; **Judy Lineback**, Christ Church Episcopal, Greenville, South Carolina; **Edward Martin**, Shepherd of the Hills United Methodist Church, Mission Viejo, California; **Charles Mathison**, Saint Paul's United Methodist Church, Louisville, Kentucky; **Alan McGuckian**, Jesuit Communication Centre, Dublin, Ireland; **Terry L. Meyer**, Alliance United Methodist Church, Fort Worth, Texas; **Steve Petty**,* Saint Andrews by the Sea United Methodist Church, San Clemente, California; **Preston Price**,* Garden Grove United Methodist Church, Garden Grove, California; **Sue Pruner**, San Luis Obispo United Methodist Church, San Luis Obispo, California; **Roland Rink**, Horizon Methodist Church, Kloofendal, South Africa; **Laura Sappington**, Calvary United Methodist Church, New

13

Albany, Mississippi; **Inez Scott**, Nestor United Methodist Church, San Diego, California; **Joe Spencer**,* Shepherd of the Hills United Methodist Church, St. George, Idaho; **Mary Dale Thomas**, Marvin United Methodist Church, Tyler, Texas; **Priscilla Van Giesen**,* United Methodist Church of the Resurrection, Leawood, Kansas; **Jean Wright-Elson**, First United Methodist Church, San Diego, California; **Rhea Zackich**, Garden Grove United Methodist Church, Garden Grove, California.

Why Pray Together?

Maxine Bolden writes that in her prayer group, "Our individual relationships with God have bloomed, our identities in Christ have changed, our accountability to each other and our families/relationships have become more certain, and we have found new ways to worship, praise, and pray to God."

The popular image of prayer consists of an individual with eyes closed, head bowed, perhaps kneeling with hands folded, silently communing with God in the privacy of his or her soul. Prayer is inherently an experience of open communion between a human spirit and the divine spirit of God.

Jesus prayed by himself. He left his disciples behind while he went off to quiet places and communicated privately with God. He took his disciples with him to the garden of Gethsemane, but he went on beyond where they rested so that he could pray alone.

But Jesus also prayed with people. He taught his disciples to pray. The prayer he taught them used plural pronouns, assuming that the prayer would be prayed by a community: "*Our* Father . . . give *us*, forgive *us*, bring *us, . . .*" (Matt. 6:9-13). Christian prayer modeled on this witness of Jesus has been a shared experience throughout the history of the church. Christian people have always prayed together. It is part of who we are.

When the first followers of Jesus in the early church prayed together, that community experienced power. Luke tells the stories in the Acts of the Apostles. These young believers met together in an environment that was not hospitable to this new faith. In response to danger and threat, they "raised their voices together to God" (Acts 4:24). Then, "when they had prayed, the place in which they were gathered together was shaken; and they were all filled with the Holy Spirit and spoke the word of God with boldness" (4:31). Later, when Peter was put in prison, Luke reports, "the church prayed fervently to God for him" (Acts 12:5). The doors of the prison were opened.

Christian people in the contemporary church continue to pray together and to experience power in their prayers. Jesus said it would be so. Talking to his disciples, he said, "Again, truly I tell you, if two of you agree on earth about anything you ask, it will be done for you by my Father in heaven. For where two or three are gathered in my name, I am there among them" (Matt. 18:19-20).

Praying together provides the following benefits:

1. Praying together enables Christians to claim Christ's promise of power through shared prayer. The Christian life is a pilgrimage, a journey of faith. When geese migrate, they fly in formation as a flock. The combined force of their wings as they share the work of cutting through the air moves the flock more smoothly and swiftly than if each individual bird flew alone. Sharing together in prayer gives added power to the prayers of each person. Jesus promised that where two or three are gathered together in his name, he would be there among them. Praying together is built on this promise of his presence and his power.

2. Praying with others encourages the practice of prayer. The pace of contemporary life hinders many people from developing a regular pattern of personal prayer. Sunday worship services provide worshipers a setting for praying at least once a week. A prayer group gives a structure in which to focus on prayer. Covenant groups foster accountability for praying regularly. A prayer chain prompts intercession for others. By gathering to pray together we call one another to prayer, and we open ourselves to God's presence with us and among us in ways that we might not otherwise do.

17

In reporting on the impact of a prayer group experience, people use the words *inspiration* and *encouragement*. Praying with others, they say, helps them persevere in the holy habit of personal prayer, with the end result of a deeper relationship with Jesus Christ.

3. Praying together helps people learn to pray and to expand their ideas about prayer. Children, young people, new Christians, all of us learn to pray as we hear the words, observe the body language, and feel the spirit of someone who prays with us. Faith in the power of prayer can be nurtured by the experience of seeing how God works in response to the prayers of others. We can expand and enrich our prayers by hearing the images others use and observing the approach they take in prayer. The agenda for prayer grows as we learn about other persons' perspectives and insights and share their experience in communing with God. We can improve private prayer by what we learn in shared prayer.

4. Praying the prayers of the church together connects us with one another, our heritage, and the universal church. Praying together the prayers that have been

shaped and tested over time in Christian worship helps individual Christians to grow into the faith of the church. These prayers become part of who we are at the deepest levels of our being. This shared experience strengthens our identity as part of the church community and, in turn, strengthens the church for its mission and ministry.

5. Shared prayer adds power to the work of intercession. Christians dare to believe that God needs and wants our prayers, our compassionate intercession for one another and for the world. Through our prayers for one another, circumstances are changed and the work of the kingdom is done. An individual may feel overwhelmed by the needs of the world, or even the needs of a single congregation, but there is strength in numbers. Individuals gain courage for the task of intercession when the community prays together, aware of Christ's presence among those gathered in his name. And the person for whom prayers are offered feels the added force of multiple prayers.

6. Praying with one another is one of the ways we "bear one another's burdens." Paul instructed the members of the early church to adopt this compassionate

lifestyle because, he said, "in this way you will fulfill the law of Christ" (Gal. 6:2). Knowing that someone else is praying with us or for us, especially if we can hear the prayers, can be a source of great encouragement, strength, and hope.

7. Praying when we are together is a witness to the value we give to prayer. When we begin our meetings with prayer, give prayer time priority, invite people to meet together for prayer, schedule family time for prayer, we make a statement that prayer is important to the life of the Christian church and to the lives of Christian people.

8. Praying together nurtures a healthy interdependence within the church. In a cultural climate that emphasizes individualism and independence, the experience of praying together builds community and encourages a climate of mutual support.

    Robert Bellah, in his book *Habits of the Heart*, talks about the extreme individualism that has come to characterize American society in recent history. Community and concern for the common welfare have fallen by the way as people pursue individual self-enhancement. When people become self-absorbed, the quality of community life is endangered, he warns. Radical individualism can have a similar impact on the church, which can become simply a place to go for what we want when we need it. But when we come together to pray with one another, we create bridges and community in the people of God.

9. Finally, some people who are naturally extroverted will find the experience of praying with others more satisfying than praying alone. The church that provides opportunities for praying with others will meet an important need for them.

Getting Started

Perhaps your congregation wants to encourage the natural inclination of Christians to pray together by providing opportunities for shared prayer. The Spirit may raise up leaders who are gifted in personal prayer and in helping members of their congregations to pray with others. Congregations may want to schedule special times and reserve special places where people can come specifically to pray together. This book is designed as an aid to those who want to help make such prayer fellowship happen.

In this resource you can explore brief descriptions of twenty-two ways in which people currently are praying together in local churches. You'll find at least one example for each, and Voices of Experience offer practical advice from real life. Administrative suggestions for successfully starting these prayer ministries and for maintaining them in good health and spirit are included. Those who want to know more may consult the Resources section.

Those who undertake to lead in any prayer ministry will find power and direction by spending time in prayer as they begin. The administration of prayer ministries is appropriately rooted in prayer.

The best place to start in developing the prayer ministry of a local congregation will be the point where you currently find yourselves. Prayers are part of congregational worship. Meetings are often opened and closed with prayer. Those going through difficult times or facing crisis situations routinely request prayers. A group in the church may have completed a study of prayer. Other settings and patterns where people pray together may be firmly in place. Summarizing what you already do and evaluating the value of each component are good ways to launch your planning.

With a clear picture in hand of where you are, you can begin by building on what you do best. Kennon L. Callahan, in his best-selling book *Twelve Keys to an Effective Church*, points to the power and energy that spontaneously feed efforts built on something that is already going well. "Power for the future," he says, "is found in claiming our strengths, not in focusing on our weaknesses and shortcomings."[1] Look at the settings where people pray together in the church and identify all the places where people experience the miracle of communication between God's spirit and their spirit. Where in the prayer life of your congregation do people feel spiritually nurtured, strengthened, and built up in faith by praying with others? When people express gratitude to others for prayers offered on their behalf, where do they direct this gratitude? What settings for prayer seem to attract people or keep them coming back? Identify established prayer settings that are going well. Claim these strengths.

Resources in this book will offer ideas about how you might improve what your church already does well and build on that foundation. Then new ministries can be added to reflect interests already expressed or to supplement successful dimensions of the church's life. Look for the places in the life of your parish where God's spirit moves and expand the opportunities for people to pray together in support of those current ministries.

The Rolling Hills Church had a very successful parish nurse ministry through the volunteer services of a retired nurse practitioner one day a week. Eight laypersons had been trained in caring ministries through the Stephen Ministry program. The leader of the congregation's contemporary music group recently had experienced a service of healing prayer at a conference on worship. She was eager to begin a similar prayer service at Rolling Hills for which her group would provide music. The combination of resources clicked. The parish nurse, the Stephen Ministers, and the musicians put their heads together and soon were able to offer a monthly Wednesday evening service of healing prayer to the community.

The launching process for a new prayer ministry is crucial to its long-term success. A lot of "up-front" work makes a good solid start possible. Based on her experience as a local church pastor, Dee Hazen suggests the following: "Be sure that there is a felt need and a clear vision for meeting that need. Do your homework at the beginning in terms of details. Get feedback promptly and rework the design until things are flowing smoothly. The ministry then can move on its own momentum."

A sermon series on prayer strategically timed in relation to the beginning of either a prayer study or a new prayer ministry can stimulate congregation-wide interest and motivate involvement. Similarly, a study program on prayer can be an effective starting point for strengthening or expanding the prayer life of the congregation. Resources described in the chapter on prayer classes and in the bibliography can serve as training tools for those interested in offering foundational studies. Frequent study opportunities on the subject of prayer will maintain the health and energy of a congregation's prayer life. New Christians, new members, and long-term members whose interest in prayer has been stimulated by a life experience will welcome a chance to join an ongoing ministry that aids them in learning to pray.

A small group of church leaders may set the direction for prayer ministry by first engaging in their own study. Their expanded and enriched prayer life can generate the vision that motivates others in the congregation to become interested and involved. Beginning with the leaders is generally a good strategy. From the initial stages, the pastor and key lay leaders of the congregation need to be informed and involved. Their connection with the process will help make the prayer ministries an organic part of the congregation's life and will add stability and strength to what is developed.

A new prayer ministry may get off to a better start if a few people test it, adapt it to the local situation, and then publicize the ministry by enthusiastically relating their firsthand experience to the larger community. Two or three people may gather to pray with a purpose and a format and later invite others to join them. This approach gives leaders time to work out the kinks in the ministry and to develop a comfort level before expanding participation to a larger group.

One deadly temptation is to try to do too many new things at once. A book full of ideas about interesting ways to pray together may add to that temptation! Ken Callahan offers these general recommendations: Begin with one new initiative that builds on a strength, that utilizes gifts and resources already available, or that responds to a clearly felt need. Identify and train leaders, and arrange the necessary support systems to make the new venture effective. Integrate this new dimension of prayer life into the ongoing life of the church before moving on to another level of prayer enrichment.[2]

1 Prayer in Congregational Worship

It is Worldwide Communion Sunday, and as I kneel at the Communion rail, I am aware of the vast community of Christians around the world who join in prayer as they receive the Communion elements during the twenty-four hours of this day. In my mind's eye, I can see Earth as it moves through space. It is as if a band of warm glow from the prayers of God's people at worship sweeps across the surface of the globe as the hours of worship pass. I am glad for this special day of remembrance of what happens every week.

On an average Sunday morning, millions of Christians gather to pray with one another in churches around the world. On Christmas and Easter, millions more join them. In the local congregation, with rare exceptions, more people participate in the regular worship services than in any other ministry of the church. "Prayer is at the heart of worship," says *The Book of Order* of the Presbyterian Church (USA).[3] When we worship together, we pray together. The sheer number of people involved in congregational worship services means those services are foundational to thinking about opportunities for shared prayer.

Congregational worship is also foundational in terms of the focus and direction of the life and ministry of a local church. The attitude of the congregation toward prayer in all aspects of its life will reflect the attitude toward prayer in its primary worship services. Is prayer real or perfunctory? Is it central to the service or just part of the support structure in which "more important" elements like preaching and music are presented? What value do the leaders put on the prayer time in the service? The quality of prayer in corporate worship will be a key factor in determining the quality of other opportunities for praying together in a local church.

Services of congregational worship typically offer the widest range of experiences of prayer in the life of a congregation. Here is where the whole spectrum of prayer can be experienced in a meaningful flow. Praise, confession, thanksgiving, dedication, petition, supplication, and silent prayers are all standard parts of corporate Christian worship. The balance provides a good basic diet for spiritual nutrition. Regular participation in congregational worship prevents anorexia of the soul and feeds our spiritual hunger with the essentials for life. A natural starting place for consideration of the prayer ministries of a local church is with a look at prayer in congregational worship.

The United Methodist Book of Worship describes a basic pattern for worship for use in developing orders of worship. The service begins with *Entrance,* when people come together in God's name with greetings, music, prayer, and praise. *Proclamation and Response* follow, employing the pattern of the synagogue service in Jesus' day. The scriptures are read and proclaimed with responses, including acts of commitment and faith and offerings of concerns, prayers, gifts, and service. The third step is *Thanksgiving and Communion,* including prayers of thanksgiving and the celebration of the Lord's Supper. *Sending Forth* with God's blessing ends the service.[4]

The Directory for Worship of the Presbyterian Church (USA) provides a similar basic pattern with five major actions centered in the Word of God: (1) gathering around the Word; (2) proclaiming the Word; (3) responding to the Word; (4) sealing of the Word (sacraments); and (5) bearing and following the Word into the world.[5]

The two disciples who walked with Christ on the road to Emmaus experienced the flow of this pattern of worship (Luke 24:13-35), explains the United Methodist *Book of Worship*:

As on the first day of the week the two disciples were joined by the risen Christ, so in the power of the Holy Spirit the risen and ascended Christ joins us when we gather. As the disciples poured out to him their sorrow and in so doing opened their hearts to what Jesus would say to them, so we pour out to him whatever is on our hearts and thereby open ourselves to the Word. As Jesus "opened the Scriptures" to them and caused their hearts to burn, so we hear the Scriptures opened to us and out of the burning of our hearts praise God. As they were faced with a decision and responded by inviting Jesus to stay with them, so we can do likewise. As they joined the risen Christ around the table, so can we. As Jesus took, blessed, broke, and gave the bread just as the disciples had seen him do three days previously, so in the name of the risen Christ we do these four actions with the bread and cup. As he was "made known to them in the breaking of bread," so the risen and ascended Christ can be known to us in Holy Communion. As he disappeared and sent the disciples into the world with faith and joy, so he sends us forth into the world. And as those disciples found Christ when they arrived at Jerusalem later that evening, so can we find Christ with us wherever we go.[6]

EXAMPLES

An Order of Worship using the basic pattern. An Order of Worship derived from the basic pattern is given in *The United Methodist Book of Worship*. Several elements of the order are described specifically as prayers, which are given themes or topics. These prayers are highlighted in bold print here, with the understanding that the entire order is a form of prayer as worship.

Entrance

- Gathering
- Greeting and hymn

Opening Prayers and Praise
(These may include a prayer of the day, a prayer of confession and act of pardon, or a litany or responsive prayer combined with an act of praise.)

Proclamation and Response

Prayer for Illumination
(The blessing of the Holy Spirit is invoked upon the reading, preaching, hearing, and doing of the Word.)

- Scripture
- Sermon
- Response to the Word

Concerns and Prayers
(Petitions, intercessions, thanksgivings, and blessings may be expressed in a pastoral prayer.)

Confession, Pardon, and Peace
(This may include a call to confession by the leader, a prayer of confession by the people, silence, words of assurance or declaration of pardon by the leader, and a response by the people.)

Offering (with **Prayer of Dedication**)

Thanksgiving
(Without Holy Communion)

Prayer of Thanksgiving

The Lord's Prayer

Thanksgiving
(With Holy Communion)

Taking the bread and cup

The Great Thanksgiving
(This may include phrases specific to the season of the Christian year in which the service is conducted.)

The Lord's Prayer

- Breaking the bread
- Giving the bread and cup

Sending Forth

- Hymn or song

Dismissal with Blessing
(Given by the pastor, this blessing is addressed to the people and not to God.)

- Going forth[7]

Worship services in Christian churches around the world offer a wide range of variations on this pattern, but most include multiple forms of prayer shared in some kind of regular order for the ongoing worship of the community.

Prayers in congregational worship may be the formal liturgical prayers of the church or extemporaneous and spontaneous. They may be written and read, prayed aloud by the congregation in unison or responsively, or prayed by worship leaders on behalf of the congregation. Many prayers in congregational worship services are sung. Some are a regular part of the service, while others fit special occasions or seasons of the church year. Congregational worship commonly includes shared praying of the Lord's Prayer. The congregational worship service provides an unparalleled opportunity for involving people in a variety of prayers and ways of praying.

Weekday prayer meetings. One variation on the theme of congregational worship that deserves special mention is the weekday prayer meeting. A weekday opportunity for praying typically uses several parts of the Sunday order of worship but is more informal than the Sunday service and includes fewer components. A weekday prayer meeting focuses on singing hymns, reading and reflecting on scripture, and praying together.

Taizé prayer. In recent years, a form of congregational worship from the Taizé community in

France has grown in popularity in this country. An international Protestant community of brothers begun during World War II, the Taizé community is committed to reconciliation among Christians, among peoples, and among nations with the ultimate goal of world peace. Programs offered at the Taizé center attract people, primarily youth and young adults, from many countries. The unique meditative prayer of the community and especially the music composed and used there have traveled around the world with these visitors as they have returned to their homes.

Taizé prayer is characterized by the use of short songs repeated over and over in "meditative singing." Using just a few words of faith—such as "Prepare the way of the Lord"; "Kyrie eleison"; "Jesus, remember me . . ."—the songs serve as a way of listening to God. For participants in this special worship, the shared singing provides not only a means of becoming attentive to God in community but also an expression of the individual prayers of those who sing together. The songs become part of the participants' consciousness, something they take away with them to their home communities. Wherever they live and work, they become instruments for "praying without ceasing."

Taizé prayer combines the meditative singing with readings from scripture, a time of silence, intercessions offered with a sung response to each prayer, a litany of praise, the Lord's Prayer, and a concluding prayer. The order always includes a selection from the Psalms, which may be read or sung, and a passage from one of the Gospels. As a song is sung either before or after the reading of the Gospel lesson, candles may be lighted and brought forward to illuminate an oil lamp set on a lamp stand. This light symbolizes the love of Christ. In the midst of the darkness in our own lives and in the world, Christ's light is a "fire that never goes out."

Ideally a service of Taizé prayer is conducted in a congregation's central place of worship. Everyone, including leaders and musicians, faces in the same direction if possible to symbolize the focus on Christ. A simple worship setting with an open Bible, candles, icons, flowers, subdued lighting, places to kneel for prayer, and song sheets can be prepared with minimal effort. A guitar or keyboard instrument can support the singing for a small group. For a larger group, a small musical ensemble may be appropriate. Leaders and musicians are seldom visible, sometimes taking up places among or behind the worshipers. Taizé services are usually scheduled at times other than Sunday morning.[8]

VOICES OF EXPERIENCE

In the introduction to a book of public prayers, Harry Emerson Fosdick describes the minister's function in leading congregational prayer. In the Protestant tradition, Fosdick notes, the minister does not kneel in the chancel, facing the altar, but rather stands in the pulpit, facing the congregation. That fact symbolizes the minister's role as trying so to phrase the soul's adoration, thanksgiving, penitence, petitions, and intercessions that the people may be caught up into the minister's prayer and may themselves pray with him or her. Fosdick says,

> That is a sacred, soul-searching task. It calls for deep and sympathetic insight into human need, for sensitive awareness of both individual and social problems, and for faith in God's grace and mercy, and it demands dedicated and careful preparation as much as does the preaching of a sermon.[9]

Ruth Duck, in her book *Finding Words for Worship*, offers the following advice for those who write prayers for use in congregational worship:

1. "Words of worship must be accessible on first hearing," she says. Keep sentence structure simple and language familiar, since people will not have time to reflect on the meaning of the words.

2. The appropriate tone for such prayer is "reverent intimacy." Tone is a matter of attitude more than of words, a joyful

expression of awe and love toward the God of love and power. The best of everyday language can communicate this attitude.

3. Consistently speak to God in prayer. "Some prayers begin by speaking *to* God," Duck notes, "and then slip into speaking *about* God as do the following words: 'We thank you, God, for coming to us in Jesus Christ, who shows us the ways of God.' To say 'who came to show us your ways' would be more consistent." Speaking to God directly helps worshipers focus attention on God.

4. Corporate prayer is not the time for announcements or sermons. Prayer for an event or activity is not an appropriate occasion for a first-time announcement of the details about it. A prayer after preaching is not the place for a sermon summary. A prayer of confession is not the time to express only one side of a controversial issue. Duck warns, "When a prayer includes more than one sentence that does not directly address God with 'you' or 'your,' preaching or teaching has probably replaced praying."

5. Prayers that are to be spoken in unison by the congregation work best when they use common rhythms and words

with few syllables. Duck suggests that anyone writing congregational prayers say them aloud and then edit them to be sure people will be able to pray easily in unison.

6. The unison prayer must be "something the whole congregation can say honestly," she says. "The goal is not to impose one's beliefs and experiences but to walk alongside other Christians, giving voice to shared experiences and challenges of life and faith."[10]

Those who study and craft contemporary worship services differ in opinion about length and style of the pastoral prayer. Some people prefer using several short prayers on separate themes scattered through the service. Others favor a longer, more inclusive pastoral prayer. In this latter case, a sung prayer chorus or verse of a prayer hymn just before the prayer, as well as a time of silence for personal prayer after the spoken prayer, can deepen the experience of communion with God for the congregation.

2 Prayer Chain

Steve Petty tells the story of an experience as a young pastor with a church prayer chain: "Gus was very sick. Already in his eighties, he had several health problems. He was diabetic. He had heart problems, high blood pressure, and high cholesterol. He had been transferred from the hospital to a convalescent care unit to die. He now had gangrene in both legs. As his pastor, I came to call. Gus told me that they wanted to amputate both his legs and that he was going to die. I offered to share his concerns with the prayer chain of our church. Out of habit, I asked Gus and his wife what they wanted to pray for. Thelma, his wife, responded quickly. 'I want him to get well so that I can take him home.' Gus wanted to pray for a miracle. He would agree to the amputations. He wanted to pray that the surgery would work and his circulation return, and that he would be able to go home and harvest his garden. I left the convalescent unit and started the request through the prayer chain. A week later, Gus went home. Two weeks later, he was in church in a wheelchair. At the end of the summer Gus harvested his garden and brought me a sack of beets and zucchini."

One of the most frequently used ways for praying together in a congregation outside the regular worship service is the prayer chain. A trusted and responsible official starter passes a request for prayer, by telephone or e-mail, to a roster of people who have agreed to pray for those who request prayer and to relay the request to the next person on the list. Prayer chains grow out of the perception that one of the most caring and helpful things we can do for one another in times of need is to pray. The prayer chain is crisis-oriented and time-sensitive. Members of a prayer chain respond immediately to a need. With a minimum amount of time and effort, a significant number of people can be involved in the prayer chain. Praying separately wherever they are when they receive the message, members know they are part of a community of prayer connected like the links of a chain.

A prayer chain can be small and simple. The members of a modest-sized group agree on an order in which the word will be passed if any member of the group has a special need. When someone in the group wants the prayer support of the others, he or she calls the starter person and the word goes out. One church reported that developing a number of small prayer chains had helped maintain the level of caring in the congregation during a time of rapid growth.

Prayer chains can be larger and more complex. A congregation may develop several kinds of prayer chains for special purposes or to fit the schedules of people willing to be on the chain. Some people may be more comfortable praying for friends and neighbors, while others are interested in praying for needs in the community or in the world. A prayer chain organized to include all members of the congregation emphasizes the mutual responsibility of members to care for one another in the Christian community. Whatever its size or practical requirements, the chain is simply a way of linking those who have a shared concern in shared prayer and of doing so quickly and efficiently. However, when the chain becomes more complex either in size or assignment, training and supervision are advisable.

Even the simplest prayer chain benefits from a clear set of procedures and policies. Members of the chain need to understand their responsibilities and to hear suggestions on how to keep the chain functioning effectively. Members of the group or congregation need to know how to communicate their prayer requests and to understand what they can expect from this group. The following questions may help in designing and operating an effective chain:

- How does someone get a prayer request on the chain?

- Who starts the chain?

- Will the prayer chain define what kind of prayer requests are appropriate for the chain?

- During what hours will the starter person be available?

- In the starter's absence, whom does one call?

- What information regarding a prayer request do members of the prayer chain need to receive? Will all requests be considered confidential? Will some requests be public information? How will chain members know what is confidential?

- How does a prayer-chain member respond if the next person on the chain is not at home or available? if a relative of the next "link" answers the call?

- Is it appropriate to call or write notes to the person who has made the prayer request?

- How will members of the chain assure accuracy in communication of the prayer request as it is passed along?

- How will the starter person know that the message has reached the end of the chain?

- Will members of the prayer chain receive feedback or updates on the status of those for whom they have prayed?

- How are members added or retired from the prayer chain?

- What training is provided for new members?

E X A M P L E S

Joe Spencer organizes the prayer chain in his church on just two levels. On the first level, a covenant intercessory prayer group known as the Prayer Warriors intercedes for confidential prayer requests. They pass on to a larger group of intercessors the nonconfidential prayer requests that have been brought to the group. Each Prayer Warrior has a Prayer Supporter Call List of not more than five people. In this structure, the original request is repeated only twice: once to the Prayer Warrior and once by that person to each Prayer Supporter. This design reduces the likelihood that information will be distorted in the process of transfer from person to person.

Steve Petty's congregation designates chains according to the time availability of those on the chain. For the regular chains, calls are not passed after 9:00 P.M. A Night Owl Chain is available until midnight, and the Extreme Team is available around the clock. A Cyber Chain operates in broadcast mode via e-mail. The request does not need to be passed on to anyone, since everyone on the chain receives the original message directly from the starter simultaneously. Each person picks up the message at his or her convenience. The prayer chains follow a list of DOs and DON'Ts:

- DO make it a point to have a pen and paper near your phone.

- DO take exact note of the prayer request.

- DO ask the caller to repeat the request if you do not hear some part of it.

- DO repeat the request back to the sender to verify that all of your information is correct.

- DON'T ask questions beyond the information given; it will not be available.

- DON'T spend time making comments on the request.

- DON'T call the people being prayed for to tell them you are praying.

- DO immediately stop what you were doing and offer a prayer for that need. You may pray in any way that suits you, silently or aloud, head bowed or looking up, kneeling or standing. God will hear all prayers, but only if they are offered.

- DO call the next person on the prayer chain as soon as you have finished praying.

VOICES OF EXPERIENCE

❖ The telephone prayer chain will work best if the number of persons on the chain is fewer than ten. Some recommend a limit of five or six people. Generally, reporting churches found it difficult to keep the message accurate and to get the message through to everyone on a long chain. A long chain may also slow down the delivery of the message. Multiple, shorter chains offer an attractive alternative to one long chain. Where the entire congregation or a large group is involved, the chain may be organized with a central core of people on the chain, each of whom calls four or more other persons.

❖ Support and affirmation for chain members bolster morale and interest. Thank-you messages from those for whom they have prayed may be shared with all members of the chain. Positive publicity about the chain in church publications creates a favorable image. An occasional meeting can provide inspiration, information, training, and feedback.

❖ Prayer chains require maintenance and adjustment or repair at intervals. Leadership meetings at least annually foster well-tuned machinery. Devise a method to assure all links on the chain are passing the message along accurately and promptly and take remedial action when problems appear. To find out whether the chain has been completed correctly, ask the last person on the chain to call the starter and relay the message that has been received.

❖ The starter may add to the description of the situation or need a specific suggestion for the content of the prayer. When a request for prayer is made, the starter may ask the person making the request, "How can we pray for you or for this other person or situation? What is your wish or your best hope?" A simple summary of what to include in the prayer is communicated with the prayer request. Prayer suggestions are kept short, simple, and specific.

❖ Some members of a prayer chain may want to reach out with more than their prayers to persons making prayer requests. Those experienced with prayer chains recommend developing clear guidance about what is appropriate. In some churches, one or more members of the chain or a special team takes responsibility for writing notes or making other contacts so that those who request prayer know people are praying and caring, but they are not inundated with contacts.

❖ Crises or emergencies in the community or in the world may be lifted up through the prayer chain as a way of calling the congregation to prayer for others between Sunday worship services.

3 Intercessory Prayer Group

Inez meets with a small group of women who gather on Tuesday mornings to offer intercessory prayer and to deepen and expand their individual prayer lives through study, meditation, and experimenting with a variety of prayer forms. The room is set up with a circle of chairs around a small table holding one or more candles. During the first thirty minutes, each woman relates where she is on her own journey. As the women listen to one another and to the Spirit, they determine how to spend their prayer time. Using the prayer cards turned in during Sunday worship and other concerns of which they are aware, they offer intercessory prayer in a variety of ways. Sometimes each one takes a card and reads it aloud. Sometimes one person reads the cards and others add information. Sometimes they conversationally name those in need. They pray aloud or silently as the Spirit leads the group. Occasionally Inez will lead a guided prayer, asking each person to allow the Spirit to reveal a person for whom they are to pray, holding that person up for God's healing presence and asking what God calls them to do for the person. Music is used for centering as appropriate. The last half hour is personal growth time during which group members try a variety of ways to praise and thank God and to experience God in deeper ways. When there is a need, they practice laying on of hands, praying as a group for each person present. Inez sometimes uses guided meditations.

Joyce has been coming to the group for a year and a half. She is amazed that she can now pray aloud for other people. She is now able to offer up names from the prayer cards and ask God for help in healing or to give thanks for blessings. Everyone prays in turn, but sometimes the prayers can be offered silently. Surprised at how much she has grown spiritually, Joyce says, "We find new doors open to us to offer God's goodness. We feel very close to one another and have a deeper regard for our congregation, our neighbors, our family, and our pastors. We have learned that by asking God's help for others, a fuller sense of God's love and help has come to our own lives. We have all changed, having now a greater sense of fulfillment and constant presence of God. We thank God for our growth!"

Diane, a young mother of preschool twins, led a prayer group for her church. On Wednesday mornings, her mother regularly came to stay with the twins, while Diane packed up her tape player and prayer guide sheets and went to the church. Six other young mothers and one of the pastors met with her for an hour and a half to read scripture, sing, and pray together. They employed a format called ACTS—Adoration, Confession, Thanksgiving, and Supplication. First they shared around the circle prayer requests for themselves and others. Using the prayer guide sheets, they moved through four steps of prayer. Beginning with adoration, described as "who God is . . . not so much what God does," they read in unison one of the biblical admonitions to praise God on the guide sheet (Pss. 8:1; 9:1; 9:2; 34:1; 34:3). All in the circle shared their praise for the day. Accompanied by taped music, they sang a praise chorus: "Let's just praise the Lord, praise the Lord, let's just lift our voice toward heaven and praise the Lord!" Next came confession with scripture (1 John 1:8, 9), a round of confession followed by a chorus—"God is so good, God is so good, God is so good. He's so good to me!" Thanksgiving followed with biblical directives (Eph. 5:20; Col. 3:15-16), expressions of thanksgiving, and a chorus—"Jesus, we just want to thank you, thank you for being so good." Supplication began with scripture (Eph. 6:18; Jas. 5:16), moved to prayers for themselves and others, and concluded with a verse of the hymn—"Have thine own way, Lord! Have thine own way!" Joining hands, the young mothers closed the session with "And all the people said AMEN." With hugs all around, they visited and then returned to their cars and the business of the day.

By far the most popular form of prayer ministry in local churches (according to research for this book) is the intercessory prayer group. As individuals, we act out our caring for others by praying for them. Congregations reveal the compassionate nature of their corporate personality by the presence of a group who lifts up intercessions for those in need. Intercessory prayer for both individuals and congregations expresses Christian identity.

Intercessory prayer has some surprising dimensions. Although intercessory prayer comes naturally and easily to most people, it also tends to raise challenging and interesting theological questions about God's nature and God's relationship to us; about how we relate to

God and to one another; about the nature of prayer—its limits and its effects; and about how best to pray. Also, while the intent of intercessory prayer groups is to serve the good of those prayed for, those who gather to pray for others may receive some of the greatest benefits. Members of intercessory prayer groups often find their faith both challenged and growing and their own spiritual lives becoming deeper and stronger. Intercessory prayer groups can easily become valuable spiritual-growth groups, particularly groups that include time for study and for reflection on what they are doing, and that, like Diane's group described above, experience several kinds of prayer during their time together.

Examples

Intercessory prayer groups come in an extensive variety of shapes and forms. Some gather just to pray. Others combine study or meditative reading of scripture with prayer. While many receive requests for prayer from people outside the group, some limit their intercessions to the needs of which they are personally aware or to requests from members of their church communities. Others pray for the world.

Churches receive requests for prayer in a variety of ways. Cards placed in a convenient location in the Sunday worship services (pew racks, in the bulletin) encourage worshipers to write their requests and leave them for pickup (in the offering plate or a basket in the narthex, for example). Telephone requests are directed to pastors, prayer group leaders, or designated voice mailboxes. A growing number of churches offer e-mail addresses and church Web-site space for submitting prayer requests.

Simple prayer-request forms ask just the name of the person for whom prayer is desired and the specific petition. Others add a box to check to request that a short note of encouragement be sent to the person in addition to the prayer. Ron Hopperton reported the following: "Over half of the requests coming in now request these notes. This has become a wonderful sub-ministry in itself that has really appealed to our congregation. We now have our own stationery and send prayer-o-grams or brief letters." Priscilla Van Giesen's church provides a large card for registering prayer requests. The card lists several categories covering a broad range of possibilities for prayer that encourages people to think beyond the limits of health problems and major crises: Grief/Loss, Child/Teen, Employment/Financial, Spiritual Guidance, Marriage/Family Relationships, as well as Health/Healing.

John Clifford and his congregation developed five "circles of concern" to help shape their intercessions and to keep persons requesting prayer from focusing too narrowly on their closest needs. These circles of concern are (1) self, (2) family, (3) community (people you know), (4) nation (people you don't know personally), and (5) world (that is, groups of people and all creation). John initiated the congregation's intercessory prayer group with a five-week study. Each week of study developed one circle of concern. The group looked at prayers of intercession from various traditions that dealt with the given area. As group members moved out from themselves into the wider circles, they began to identify how they were connected to the people and events in each circle, enabling them to pray with greater conviction. They discovered that bringing newspapers to the group sessions helped remind them of needs in the wider world.

Joe Spencer's intercessory prayer group developed a Prayer Focus List of universal concerns about which members wanted to pray. Each month the group selects from the list one or two concerns on which to spend intense prayer time. The ongoing list includes such concerns as prison ministries, those in chronic pain, broken families, people waiting for organ transplants, international students away from families, people who are disliked, hate groups, people contemplating suicide. The group picks new subjects for the constantly growing list during the first meeting of the month, but new concerns may be added at any time.

Intercessory prayer group members often leave their meetings with a list of those for whom the group has prayed, having committed to continue praying daily for those requests over a set period of time. Some intercessory groups also pray for persons who have not requested prayer. Joe Spencer's group at each meeting draws the names of four persons or families from the congregational membership list. Each person or family receives a letter explaining that the prayer group will be praying for the person or family during the coming week, beginning on Sunday. The selected persons are invited to notify the prayer group leader of any requests for prayer. Otherwise, they are told, "we will be lifting you up as a whole and healthy child of God."

Dee Hazen's intercessory prayer group meets for an hour once a week. She brings prayer requests from the congregation to the group. Beginning with praise and confession, they intercede for the church staff by name, for the church's ministries, for missionaries, for the ill and shut-ins, for those who need peace and guidance, for marriages, and for the membership of the congregation (using pages out of the directory). One person in the group takes responsibility to pray aloud for each category. Other members may add to that prayer as they wish. The group closes with a time of general prayer and a time for silence.

Homebound, nursing-home, and snowbird members make up an intercessory prayer team at Asbury United Methodist Church in Michigan. Fifteen people were recruited to serve as Partners in Praise and Prayer. In a special commissioning service with their pastor, they were prayed for and received an olive wood cross, a certificate, and a large-print Bible. Monthly they receive a letter from the pastor stating special concerns for intercession. While physical limitations may reduce their opportunities to participate in the life of the church in many ways, older members of a congregation may be among the most spiritually mature and experienced pray-ers of the community. They bring rich life experience and accumulated wisdom to the task of praying for others. Involvement in the intercessory prayer ministry takes advantage of their gifts and highlights their value in the church. Being part of the intercessory prayer team of the church also provides opportunities for older members to continue growing spiritually even while experiencing physical decline.

One church gave the name "Praying Together Separately" to such an intercessory prayer group in which members pray as a community although they are apart physically. Kathy L. Grecco describes a time of crisis in her congregation when several members agreed to pray for the church and those involved in the crisis every day at the same time wherever they were. The entire congregation of another church is invited to participate in "praying together separately" for one another in a program that uses the church directory as the prayer list. Shirley Hutchison writes, "On the day when the program begins, each member of the congregation is encouraged to pray for themselves and their family. Every day after that they move down the directory list and pray for whoever is next until they pray all the way through the directory. In this way, everybody can know that someone in the congregation of their church may be praying for them that day." The church newsletter offers this suggested prayer:

> Oh God, to whom all hearts are open, all needs known, hear my prayer for [Name]. Surround [Name] with your love and provide whatever he/she needs today. Protect [Name] from evil, forgive his/her sins, and heal his/her body and spirit. My prayer turns to praise upon my lips for your bountiful love, and I thank you for the presence of [Name] in my circle of love. Amen.

Mary Dale Thomas describes a combination model, a prayer group that gathers weekly at her church. After time together to review the prayer requests, the group divides into small groups of two to five. Each group takes a section of the prayer list, goes to a different corner of the room, and prays quietly for the requests. The sound of several voices praying at the same time is not distracting but encouraging and comforting.

The Upper Room Living Prayer Center initiated a nationwide network of intercessory-prayer groups in 1977. The center charters groups of adults and youth in local churches and communities, then sends them requests for prayer that come into the center from around the nation and the world. The groups are called Covenant Prayer Groups.

V O I C E S   O F   E X P E R I E N C E

❖ Praying aloud in a group is an intimidating prospect for many people. Pat Griffith decided to gently lead members of her Bible study group past that fear. For the first several weeks of each new class, members closed the session by recording in their workbooks a prayer concern requested by each member. The ground rules stated that the concern be for oneself, not for others. Additional concerns were always allowed. After several weeks, Pat surprised the class by inviting them to offer a spoken prayer for the person to their left. Assured that no one expected an eloquent style, they were to lift up the concern simply in their own words. Pat prayed first, each person had a turn, and Pat concluded the prayer. Reporting that she has led several groups in this process, always with profound results, Pat says she has never had a member refuse to try or even have much difficulty. "There is usually a little grumbling, but people recognize the assignment as being simple, specific, and doable. With the first attempt, these simple spoken prayers are beautiful; by the second week, they are eloquent. Soon others are beginning and concluding the prayer. There is power in hearing someone pray for you by name, usually with a reference such as 'my sister Kathy' or 'my brother Michael.' A strong bond develops among the members almost instantly. And we end up with a whole new group of prayerful leaders who can pray verbally in a group."

A variation of this plan is the "squeeze-hand prayer." Members of a group led by Pam Abbey join hands. Pam says a short sentence prayer and then squeezes the hand of the person to her right. That person may then add a short prayer aloud or silently or may choose to pass and just squeeze the next hand. When the prayer comes around full circle, the leader closes or leads the group in the Lord's Prayer. Most people will loosen up considerably after they have done this a few times. By listening to others, they begin to realize that prayer does not have to be eloquent. They can be as brief as they want. The subjects of the prayers run the gamut—from seeking wisdom to handle issues they confront to gratitude for getting the garden weeded.

❖ An intercessory prayer group may find itself becoming simply a support group. A negative spirit can develop if the sharing becomes a gossip session or the conversation deteriorates into comparing notes in the vein of "ain't it awful?" To safeguard against this tendency, set the time of petition and intercession in a context of praise and thanksgiving. Sue Pruner reflects on her experience: "I think that prayer is more to the point if first we give ourselves to praise and thanksgiving for what God has done for us. Lately I've come to think that the purpose of praise is not so much to please God as it is to straighten us out. When we offer praise, we are recognizing who God is and what God has done; we are not taking credit for things. We are getting a clearer perspective on who we are in relation to God. It is truly wonderful to focus on God for a while instead of on ourselves, our wants, and our problems. Having done that, we can then turn to requests, matters we want to hold up in prayer of deep concern. I do think that these should be coupled with thanksgiving, knowing that the prayers are heard and that God will do something, although it is likely not exactly what we expect or are thinking of. It does take faith to thank God for an answer we do not yet see but are confident is in the offing."

❖ Todd C. Karges recommends printing the day and time of intercessory prayer-group meetings in church publications, so people will be aware of the group's presence and make their requests known.

❖ Notes of encouragement from the intercessory prayer group can be meaningful if carefully worded and written so as to convey a genuine personal touch. I received such a note during a time of crisis from Sheryl K. Hartley, which read, "God bless you on your good days, and carry you 'on eagle's wings' on the bad days. You are in my daily prayers." Another said: "During this difficult time in your life, know that God feels your pain and wants you to draw on divine grace for comfort. You are never alone. Love, Sheryl." Both letters "hit the spot" and seemed custom-designed for the day when they arrived in the mail.

4 Prayer Vigil

Tyler had been intrigued when he read an announcement in the church newsletter about a prayer vigil to be held on Ash Wednesday. The sanctuary would be open for twelve hours, from 7:00 A.M. to 7:00 P.M., and members of the congregation would be in prayer there for the entire time. Twenty-four people were needed to sign up for a thirty-minute shift each. The vigil would conclude thirty minutes before the annual Ash Wednesday service at 7:30 P.M. in that same space. Tyler liked the idea of launching the season of Lent with this concentrated period of prayer in the sanctuary. But who would be willing to sign up to pray in the sanctuary for such a long time? He could not imagine doing it himself. He hoped that some of the more saintly members of the congregation would do this special task on behalf of all of them.

But on Sunday morning after the service, Tyler discovered in conversation over coffee that his friend Joe was signing up for the prayer vigil. Joe, of all people! Joe's schedule was, if anything, more busy than his own. How could he take the time? And what would Joe know about praying for thirty minutes nonstop? But here was Joe telling him that it was a great experience and that Tyler ought to sign up and give it a try. "You'll be surprised,"

Joe said. "I did it last year and the time just flew by. In fact, I found that I needed to stay longer than the thirty minutes, so I stayed even after the next person came. The sanctuary is quiet. Candles are lighted. A table is set up with Bibles and suggested scriptures to read prayerfully to help you get ready for Lent. Hymnals are there, too, with suggested prayer hymns to read. A prayer guide is also provided for you to use. A blank notepad is on the table, and people who come to pray can record names and situations they want others to pray for. People who have not signed up to cover a particular time come and go as they can and sit quietly and pray too. Although we pray silently, we are like a relay team where each one of us passes the torch along to the next person, and together we make this sanctuary a place of prayer for twelve hours before we go into Lent. I just back up my wake-up time by thirty minutes and do my part on the way to work. You should try it, Tyler. You'll like it!"

Prayer vigils resemble relay races. People pray together for the same reason, but they take turns being on the job as the one who prays. A person may participate for the entire designated time, of course, or groups may stay together for one concentrated block of prayer time. But most frequently, individuals or small groups sign up for portions of the schedule and pray together in sequence, passing on the responsibility for the vigil at the end of each block of time. At the vigil, people pray quietly individually or aloud together. If several people are present for each block of time, a group leader may guide them through a prepared order of prayer. A printed list of suggestions for prayer will be helpful in any case.

A prayer vigil may be scheduled for twenty-four hours on one or more days or for part of one day. Normally a vigil takes place in the sanctuary or a congregation's primary worship site. A prayer vigil also may be conducted with participants praying at specific times in separate locations. In that case, each participant receives the prayer resources for the vigil ahead of time. Those taking off-site assignments to be in prayer at a specific time can also supplement a prayer vigil staffed at a central location.

Dee Hazen's church invited members of the congregation and community to write prayer requests on cards and to submit them before a prayer vigil. At one point in the order of prayer followed during each hour segment of the vigil, the person praying drew five cards from a basket marked "To Pray For" and prayed for those concerns. The person then placed the cards in a basket marked "Prayed For." When one basket was emptied, the tags on the baskets were exchanged, and the cards were drawn and prayed for again. During the vigil, each card was drawn and each request prayed for by several people.

A prayer vigil is an effective way to begin a season of the church year or to note a seasonal event in the community. A major enterprise, like the beginning of a building program or the establishment of a significant new missional outreach, can be an occasion for a prayer vigil. An emergency in the life of a member of the congregation or a major event or crisis in the world or community can be the focus of a prayer vigil. People join together to create an extended time of prayer lifted nonstop in the church building for those involved in the crisis or special situation. The length of the prayer time increases the power of the experience for those who participate. Many people who have experienced only brief prayers in community worship discover new dimensions of prayer and grow in their own prayer life as a result of investing the longer period of time in prayer required by a prayer vigil.

EXAMPLES

Vigil for the first day of school. Ken Carter pastors a church with a substantial number of families with young children. He says, "We offer a prayer vigil in the sanctuary for students, parents, teachers, and administrators on the first day of school, from 6:00 A.M. until 6:00 P.M. Folks sign up for fifteen-minute time periods. Our goal is to have continuous prayer. Parents are encouraged to place pictures of children or of adult teachers or administrators on the altar rail. By the end of the day the altar is filled with pictures. There are also readings provided: This year's scriptures were from Mark 9 and 10 (Jesus welcoming and blessing the children). Over forty persons participated this year. We also have a prayer focus for our partner school that includes a high density of underprivileged children."

Ash Wednesday prayer vigil. The following is a prayer guide for an Ash Wednesday prayer vigil designed as a time of preparation for Lent.

Aids to Meditation

Reflect on these words from The United Methodist Hymnal:

- No. 268, Prayer for Lent
- No. 492, "Prayer Is the Soul's Sincere Desire"
- Pages 785–86, Psalm 51:1-17

Suggested meditations from the Bible:

- Romans 12:1-12; Matthew 5:1-12; James 5:13-16; Psalm 100:1-5

Meditate on these words:

Prayer has been described as a time exposure of the soul to God. When film is exposed, it is changed. It reflects that to which it has been exposed. When we become open to God in prayer, we grant God the power to shape and transform us in the relationship. John Cobb speaks of the divine "field of force." When we open ourselves to God in prayer, we put ourselves in that field of force. Like metal filings in the force field of a powerful magnet, we will find ourselves attracted and creatively transformed. When we open ourselves to God, we give power to God's call forward to the vast possibilities that God offers to us.[11]

Suggestions for prayer: Hold each of the following concerns in your heart for a few moments. Add your own thoughts and images around each theme and offer these prayers to God.

I pray for the whole church of Jesus Christ, that during this season of repentance and hope we may be called to renewed obedience and faithfulness to our risen Lord. I pray for . . .

I pray for this local church—for the activities and worship services of Lent. I pray for the leaders of music and the proclaimers of the Word in worship, that the Holy Spirit's inspiration may work through them to touch our hearts and transform our lives in response to the message of the Cross. I pray for . . .

I pray for the leaders of the nations of the world, that they may govern their people with wisdom and compassion and work together for order, justice, and peace. I pray for . . .

I pray for those who are away from home as refugees or as prisoners and for those who have no home. May they find their home in you and know the peace that comes from dwelling in the house of the Lord. I pray for . . .

I pray for those who are close to me. May this season of remembrance of the love of God made known in the suffering of Christ be a time of blessing for them. I pray for . . .

I pray for those who have asked for my prayers, including those whose names are listed in the book on the table at this vigil. May God's will be done for each of them and may their lives be filled with God's blessing. I pray for . . .

I pray for *[names of individuals or groups]*.

These prayers I make in company with those who pray with me here today, and I join with them in praying the prayer that you taught us to pray, saying *[The Lord's Prayer]*.

You may list requests for prayer in the book on the table so that others following you may pray for these concerns.

V O I C E S   O F   E X P E R I E N C E

❖ Uninterrupted silence in the sanctuary or other location is essential for a vigil. The church secretary—or whoever schedules the use of space—may communicate to all staff, including custodial and music staff, the need to protect the vigil space from noise and interruptions during this time of prayer. Signs requesting quiet can be placed on all entry doors to the space where the vigil is held.

❖ The visual environment can be conducive to prayer. A simple setting without distractions is helpful, as is candlelight, which connotes active worship.

❖ Plan to have the building open, the space set up, heating or air-conditioning and lighting set for comfort, the candles lighted, and the materials in place at least fifteen minutes before the first person is scheduled to pray. Also make plans to put away prayer vigil equipment and close the building at the end of the vigil.

❖ Posting a chart of persons responsible for the various prayer times near the door of the space used for the vigil will enable participants to know whom to expect as their replacement.

❖ In scheduling participants, allow for backup support. Some people who have a flexible schedule may be willing to come anytime during the day. You may want to wait until the last day to give them a time, depending on the need. A telephone call to each person on the list within twenty-four hours of the prayer vigil's starting time to remind them of their time encourages full participation. If last-minute conflicts come up for some people, call the backup persons as replacements.

❖ As a congregation becomes experienced with prayer vigils, members may be interested in and willing to sign up for longer periods of time. An hour is not too long for many people. A single time frame does not need to be limited to one person. If two or more people request the same time, the leader can be sure to provide enough seats at the table, or a circle of chairs in the designated space, and printed resources for all who want to participate.

❖ Clear communication about the focus or purpose for the prayer vigil increases its effectiveness. Select resources designed to support the purpose.

❖ If the prayer vigil continues at night when the church property normally is deserted, think about measures to provide adequate security for participants.

5 Prayer Partners

Margaret left her pew and went forward to the front of the church to join in the dedication service for Sunday-school leaders on Christian Education Sunday. When the pastor came to her in the line, he explained that Margaret and several others being dedicated that morning were assuming an important role in the ministry of Christian education. They would be on the team as prayer partners for Sunday-school classes. The prayer partners had agreed to pray each week for the students and teachers of the classes to which they were assigned and to check once a month to see how things were going. The regular conversations with the teachers would help keep the prayers specific to the life of the class. "Prayer partners," said the pastor, "acknowledge the fact that the Holy Spirit is the real teacher in Christian education. Teachers appreciate this support and realize that everything does not depend on them."

Margaret had been a Sunday-school prayer partner before. When she was asked to participate again, she had been ready to say yes. She had good memories about the experience. "I prayed," she remembered, "that each boy and girl and each teacher might be touched—now and forever—by the Spirit's presence. I found that the spiritual responsibility of 'partnership' disciplined my daily worship." So on Christian Education Sunday, here she was at the altar, ready to go again.

Teresa Erickson knew that something was wrong. The mammogram showed nothing, but her training and experience as an ICU nurse told her that she needed medical attention to the lump she could so clearly feel. Bruce, her pastor husband, shared her concern. The biopsy told them what they had dreaded to hear. The lump was not only real—it was malignant. Surgery revealed the cancer had spread into lymph nodes, and the medical team was going to have to pull out all the resources at their command to stop the disease.

Caught up in the hectic lifestyle of a two-career marriage with one of the partners on the staff of a busy church and with two school-age children at home, Teresa and Bruce had no space in their schedule for this new reality. This disease was not what they had expected to happen to them at this stage of their lives. Stunned by shock, grief, and fear, Teresa and Bruce turned to family and Christian friends for support. One of the first places to which Bruce turned was a team of ten persons who had committed to pray for him, his family, and his ministry in this church on a regular basis. The leader of the group had met with Bruce regularly, usually monthly, to allow Bruce to share his personal concerns and needs. The leader then confided those issues to other partners on the prayer team, who prayed for Bruce. With this structure already in place, Bruce soon began to experience a sense of calm and hope and confidence that the resources for coping with this new threat would be available to him.

Teresa's friends gathered around her, offering to do something—anything—to help her during her battle *with cancer. Faced with months of chemotherapy and radiation, Teresa's emotions were fragile. She prayed for wisdom about how to best receive from the Lord the encouragement and strength she needed for this physical, emotional, and spiritual challenge. Her answer was in the deep desire of her friends to help. She felt led to invite twelve women to her home for one hour twice a month to pray with and for her. Nine months later, Teresa looked back with gratitude for this prayer support team. Faith had been tested and strengthened. Teresa's doctor was pleased. "Teresa, you have just breezed through these treatments," he told her. She gave thanks for the power of shared prayer.*

Prayer partners agree to take on responsibility for lifting in prayer a person or a group on a regular, ongoing basis. Some prayer partnerships are unilateral, as in the case of Margaret and her Sunday-school class, Bruce and his pastor's support team, and Teresa and her friends. Others are mutual arrangements, as when two friends agree to lift each other in prayer as part of their daily devotional time. The commitment can be long-term—as with the two friends—or for a specific period of time—again, as with Margaret's term of a year with her class. Some prayer partners live near each other and visit regularly. Others are geographically separated and stay in touch by telephone or mail or e-mail. Most prayer partnerships are openly acknowledged, though occasionally a prayer partner is anonymous.

A long-distance prayer partnership developed as a part of writing this book. Roland Rink, a South African Christian, read the invitation to make a contribution and e-mailed this response:

> Shalom. I have spent much time pondering and praying your request. Truth is, the creative juice just will not flow!! All I am led back to is this: "Pray for Martha Rowlett." I think that this is what God is asking of me on your behalf, so it is going to be my privilege to pray for you on a daily basis. I would appreciate it if, from time to time, you let me know if there are specifics that require prayer. I work to deadlines all the time and have some insight as to the pressure we can put ourselves under, so to begin with, I propose praying for calm for you. In Africa there is a word *Ubuntu*. It means "I am because we are." May the Holy Spirit guide and sustain you in your work. May the extended global family of Christ followers surround you with the sense of Ubuntu.
>
> We go forward,
> Roland Rink

Late in the process, when the less creative, more mundane work of writing had to be done, another e-mail from Roland came to brighten the day and make the load seem lighter.

> Greetings, Martha. Simply a short note to say you encroached into my quiet time, so I

prayed. The passage I was reading was 2 Corinthians 4, which said, "God in His mercy has given us this work to do, and so we are not discouraged."

We go forward,
Roland

E X A M P L E S

Members of a young mothers' group in Priscilla Van Giesen's church pair up as prayer partners, praying daily for each other and talking or visiting once a week to stay in touch.

High-school students are prayer partners for each other in a special weekend of spiritual formation called "Discovery," led by Melody Christolear. The senior highs lead the program for the mid highs and have mid-high prayer partners with whom they pray during the weekend. Sunday-school classes also serve as prayer partners for the young people on this occasion, with youth names being distributed to the classes beforehand. Parents are invited to be part of the program by coming to a special family prayer time with their teens.

Adults can pray for young people in the church. Some churches assign all their young people to senior-citizen prayer partners who keep the assignment for a year. In connection with a mission trip or special youth event, the seniors' prayers can focus on the time of preparation as well as the duration of the trip or event.

In the spiritual-formation program called Walk to Emmaus, members of the Emmaus Community pray for assigned individuals engaged in weekend Walk to Emmaus events both before and during the retreat.

Prayer partnership plays a role in many relationships characterized as spiritual direction or spiritual friendship. The purpose of spiritual direction is mentoring in spiritual formation, and praying together often forms a committed part of the arrangement.

The need to pray for the pastor of a church might seem self-evident, since the pastor is so important in the life of a local church. But congregation members may not think about that need. The pastor as leader is naturally vulnerable to criticism, challenge, and temptations. The hours are long and the responsibilities seemingly endless. A group of persons committed to be prayer partners for the pastor can be a source of transforming power and hope.

VOICES OF EXPERIENCE

❖ Both prayer partners will understand the expectations if they determine a term of service as prayer partners at the beginning of the agreement.

❖ Contact during the term of service as a prayer partner will keep the one who prays up to date on what to include in the prayers, as well as give the one prayed for tangible support and assurance. The one who prays may ask the prayer partner for suggestions. Usually the person prayed for welcomes the question "How can I pray for you?" And asking, "How do I need to change my prayers?" assures that the prayers grow or change as circumstances change.

❖ Delia Halverson suggests that prayer partners for Sunday-school classes use a group picture of the class as an aid to prayer. One approach to the responsibility of praying for classes is to divide the class members into five groups and to pray for one of these groups on each of the days from Monday to Friday. The prayer on Saturday can focus on the group's upcoming time together on Sunday morning.

6 Prayers for Healing

Jean Wright-Elson was praying alongside her pastor for healing with people who brought their concerns and prayer requests to the altar. The congregation had responded to the new service of healing enthusiastically, and a line formed as people waited for someone to pray with them. As parish nurse, Jean appreciated this opportunity to minister by listening, praying, and anointing, using these words: "Receive God's healing grace as I anoint you with this oil in the name of the Father, the Son, and the Holy Spirit." Out of the line emerged a tall, slender woman who looked at Jean and said in a soft, breathy voice, "I wish to be healed of my breast lump." The normal procedure was put on hold for a moment as Jean leaned forward and whispered in her ear, "I hope you are under treatment." Jean was jolted by her response: "No, this is it." Before praying with the woman, Jean quickly requested that she come to see her, which she did. Jeanette was a fifty-four-year-old divorced woman. She had noticed the lump eighteen months before she had come to the healing service, believing that if she prayed and meditated hard enough, God would heal her. She was shy and passive. Doctors intimidated her. Jean listened to her fears and her convictions about the *healing power of prayer. She encouraged Jeanette to see physicians as instruments of God's healing work and answers to our prayers for healing.*

Since finances were limited, Jeanette made an appointment for a checkup at a low-cost women's clinic. Jean went to the appointment with her, realizing that Jeanette's anxiety might prevent her from understanding what was being said to her. A mammogram revealed a suspicious lump, and a biopsy was ordered. Jean stayed with Jeannette to provide medical and spiritual support. Over the coming weeks, Jeanette moved through a decision-making process that resulted in a lumpectomy and the discovery of early-stage cancer. Soon she was undergoing chemotherapy and radiation. During this process, Jean watched Jeanette change from a self-effacing, timid person to one who began to take charge and make decisions for herself. An emotionally distant relationship with a sister evolved into a closer connection. The weekly prayer group at the church and the ministerial staff lifted Jeanette in their prayers of support. Jeanette did not have the instant, miraculous healing she had come to the service expecting, but a miracle of healing did occur.

The ministry of Jesus as reported in the Gospels included preaching, teaching, and healing. The New Testament letter of James assumes that the church of Jesus Christ will carry on his ministry of healing. So James instructs the members of the early church: "Are any among you sick? They should call for the elders of the church and have them pray over them, anointing them with oil in the name of the Lord. . . . so that you may be healed" (Jas. 5:14, 16).

In the contemporary church, the public image of faith healing has suffered from the publicity around charlatan faith healers and from the aura of a magic show in some television healing services. This public image evokes distrust in thoughtful people and leaves many people uneasy with the idea of praying for healing in the Christian community. *The United Methodist Book of Worship* speaks to this concern by setting the broader context:

> A Service of Healing is not necessarily a service of curing, but it provides an atmosphere in which healing can happen. The greatest healing of all is the reunion or reconciliation of a human being with God. When this happens, physical healing sometimes occurs, mental and emotional balance is often restored, spiritual health is enhanced and relationships are healed. For the Christian the basic purpose of spiritual healing is to renew and strengthen one's relationship with the living Christ.[12]

James K. Wagner's book *An Adventure in Healing and Wholeness* develops this broader context of prayers for healing. There he describes five kinds of health that he understands to be part of Jesus' healing ministry and that are carried on in the Christian church: (1) spiritual health, (2) physical health, (3) mental and emotional health, (4) healthy relationships, and (5) ultimate health in the resurrection following the death of the body. Recognizing the limited nature of human life and knowing that all physical healing is temporary, Christian prayers for physical healing confront death with resurrection faith and understand that in the face of physical death, spiritual life can rise to new levels of health and wholeness. Reginald Mallett also reflects on this inclusive picture of spiritual healing:

> Sometimes the human body does not respond to any kind of therapy. However, when the container in which we live is hopelessly flawed, the contents can be wonderfully whole.[13]

Praying together for healing can occur anytime and anywhere Christians pray with one another. Out of the Gospel records of the healing ministry of Jesus and the traditions of the church come several elements in addition to prayer as features of healing services:

1. *Touch, or laying on of hands.* Jesus often, though not always, touched the person he healed. For many people healing power comes through gentle, loving touch, expressed in simply holding the hand of the person for whom the prayer is made or by laying the hand on the head or shoulders of the person. In a group, several people may lay their hands on the person as prayer is offered for healing.

2. *Anointing with oil.* Touching the forehead with oil, or making the sign of the cross on a person's forehead with a finger dipped in oil, is an ancient act invoking the healing power of God. In New Testament times, people used oil to treat wounds. The Good Samaritan poured oil into the wounds of the man attacked by robbers along the road to Jericho; the disciples anointed the sick with oil and healed them (Mark 6:13); and James specifically included the practice in his instruction to the church.

3. *Communion.* The sacrament of the Lord's Supper frequently concludes a service of healing prayer as a way of responding to the gift of healing. Receiving the elements in the Lord's Supper in itself conveys healing power for many. The prayers for healing may also follow the receiving of the elements.

During a regular congregational worship service, prayers for healing may be included in the intercessory prayers offered during the service. The pastoral prayer might incorporate time for silent prayer when persons express their private, individual needs for healing, followed by a spoken prayer that lifts all the individual prayers to God. If the congregation shares joys and concerns at the prayer time, the worship leader may then summarize these in a spoken prayer. An opportunity may be provided during the time of intercessory prayers for persons to come and pray quietly at the Communion rail.

Prayer for healing with laying on of hands and anointing with oil may be offered in conjunction with the sacrament of the Lord's Supper. The logistical details will differ according to a congregation's method of serving Communion, but here are some possible scenarios. Those who desire prayers for healing can come to the last table group in a setting where the congregation comes by rows to the Communion rail. In services where the elements are served to the congregation by intinction, the Communion rail can be reserved for persons who want to kneel there and have someone pray with them and perhaps receive the laying on of hands or anointing with oil. Another option is to invite those who wish to receive these ministries to return to the altar after the benediction as others leave the service.

Special services of healing prayer may be scheduled before or after congregational worship or at other times during the week. *The Book of Worship* of The United Methodist Church offers two models for basic services of healing, including suggested scripture readings and prayers, as well as resources for ministry in special situations—divorce; addiction, substance abuse, or AIDS; life-threatening diseases; or coma or inability to communicate. Suggested hymns for services of healing prayer are listed in *The United Methodist Hymnal*, No. 943. A healing prayer ministry could include prayer teams who visit persons unable to come to church in order to lay hands on them, anoint with oil, and pray for healing. Also, retreats and camps may be centered around the themes of healing and prayer.

James Wagner suggests a three-step process when praying for healing with another person. Remember L-A-P, he says. LISTEN (L). Ask each person who comes to your prayer station, "What is your prayer concern today?" Then listen closely. ANOINT (A). Using your thumb or forefinger, make the sign of the cross on the forehead with oil. PRAY (P). Offer a brief prayer.[14] Steps two and three may be reversed, but the process always begins with listening. Wagner offers three prayer patterns:

> These hands are laid upon you in the name of the Father, the Son, and the Holy Spirit. May the power of God's indwelling presence heal you of all infirmities of mind, body, spirit, and relationships, that you may serve God with a loving heart. Amen.

> Lord Jesus Christ, strengthen and heal *[name of person]*. May your healing love and power flow into *[his or her]* life. Banish all pain, sickness, and sin. Give *[him or her]* the blessings of health

in body, mind, spirit, and relationships. We ask these things in your name and give you the glory. Amen.

Thank you, Lord Jesus, for this time of Holy Communion with you and with one another. We now lift up into your light and love *[name of person]*. Touch *[him or her]*. Bring *[him or her]* wholeness in body, mind, spirit, and relationships. For doing all of these things and more, we thank you and give you the glory. Amen.[15]

EXAMPLES

The first example comes from Carla Badgett. She describes a weekly service of prayer, healing, and Holy Communion on Tuesday evenings at her church:

At 5:15 P.M. we meet in the chapel parlor for a time of prayer. At 5:30 we begin to move around the room, taking prayer requests and getting updated on people's conditions. At 6:00 we break and move into the chapel where the organist is playing soft music. The worship opens with a responsive reading from the Psalter or a unison prayer. We sing a hymn, read scripture, have a short message, and then celebrate the sacrament of Communion. We do the full Communion liturgy, opening with a

Prayer of Confession and Assurance of Pardon (a healing act in and of itself). We also have a time of passing the peace in which we can greet others and offer them love as a part of the worship service. We use a Great Thanksgiving that is appropriate to the season. After the Lord's Prayer, we invite everyone forward to receive the elements and have private prayer time at the altar. We have found that nothing said or done expresses God's presence and action in our lives in quite the same way as Communion.

After people return to their seats we have a time for the prayers of the people, when we lift up the prayer requests that were made prior to the service and allow a time of silence for additional requests. This is followed by a hymn, and then we open the altar for prayer. Two prayer teams (two people in each team) kneel behind the altar. They have oil for anointing and Kleenex for tears. Some people pray with the prayer teams, others pray alone at the altar, and others stay in the pew for prayer. Our organist plays soft music during this time. Everyone leaves when they have finished praying (this prayer time usually lasts about a half hour). After everyone has left, the prayer partners leave, the organist snuffs the candles on the altar, and it is over until the next week. This healing ministry has blessed me in more ways than I can possibly express.

Priscilla Van Giesen's church uses a service of prayer and healing based on the Basic Pattern of Worship of The United Methodist Church:

We Gather in God's Presence

Gathering

- Music for Centering
- Welcome

Proclamation

- Songs of God's Presence
- Call to Prayer
- Prayer of Confession

God of great love and compassion, we seek your presence with hopeful and grateful hearts. In our spoken words and deepest thoughts, we lift our needs to you. In our pain and fear, our souls ache for your touch, our guilt longs for your merciful forgiveness, our disease seeks your healing. Breathe your life-giving Spirit into our wounded hearts. Through every distress of mind and body, remind us always that your presence with us is our true salvation, our genuine health and greatest joy, even now as we pray silently before you. Amen.

- Silent/Listening Prayer
- Words of Assurance

Hear the Good News! The Lord says to each one of us, "You are my chosen and beloved one. I call you by name; you are mine. Know that I have forgiven you and my presence is ever with you." This is God's covenant and promise to us through Jesus Christ, by the power of the comforting Holy Spirit.

- Song of Preparation
- Living Word of Scripture
- Spoken Word

RESPONSE

- Prayer for Healing and Wholeness
- The Lord's Prayer

COMMUNION

- Thanksgiving over the Oil and Consecration of Elements

At this time you are invited to receive Holy Communion. Anointing will be available as you kneel at the prayer rail after receiving Communion. Additionally, you will be given the opportunity to have someone pray with you for your specific needs and concerns. This is optional and you should feel free to decline if you so choose. As you return to your seat, please be in silent prayer and meditation until all have been served and received anointing.

GOING FORTH

- Song of Blessing
- Benediction
- Postlude

VOICES OF EXPERIENCE

❖ Prayers for healing and services of healing can be a dimension of a congregation's larger health ministry, which might be affiliated with a parish nurse program, Stephen Ministry, or caring ministry program. Connection to an already established structure in the church's life can impart stability and strength to healing ministries.

❖ Instructions, interpretation, and explanation at each step along the way in an initial service of healing prayer help people understand what is going on and how to act. The Presbyterian Directory for Worship recommends, "When a service for wholeness includes anointing and the laying on of hands, these enacted prayers should be introduced carefully in order to avoid misinterpretation and misunderstanding. Healing is to be understood not as the result of the holiness, earnestness, or skill of those enacting the prayers, or of the faith of the ones seeking healing, but as the gift of God through the power of the Holy Spirit."[16]

❖ Allow plenty of time in a service of healing prayer for people to kneel at the rail and pray. Plan for a minimum of fifteen minutes.

❖ It is wise to ask permission before laying on of hands or even holding a person's hand for prayer. Touch should be light and gentle.

❖ Traditionally olive oil is used for anointing with oil during a service.

❖ When serving as a leader in a service of healing prayer, remember that you are not the healer. God is the Healer; you are simply there to share and care.

7 Prayer Before and During Worship Services

Mary Liz Kehoe describes a morning at her church, where people pray on Sunday mornings for the worship services: "The 8:30 service is over. David visits with friends over coffee and then goes by the Sunday-school classrooms to pick up his two sons, Will and Ben. Before going home, he and the boys stop by the church parlor to pray for the worship service that will begin soon. In the parlor, a kneeling bench is ready with a copy of the bulletin for the day's worship service and a few prayer resources. David kneels on the bench. Using the bulletin, he prays aloud for those who will be leading the service and for those who will be attending. The boys stand by their dad and pray silently with him. After a few minutes of silent prayer, the three head home. On the way out of the building, they meet a young couple who joined the church last Sunday. The membership orientation included an invitation to come by the parlor on Sunday mornings to pray for the worship services of the church, they explain. They see this practice as a way to become involved very quickly and easily in serving their new church. So, on their second Sunday as members, they are here to pray.

A congregation's weekly worship is central to its life and ministry. Important things happen during this time. Human beings lead, human beings worship, and the Holy Spirit is present among them to transform what happens into the work of the kingdom. Scheduled prayer time focused on the worship service and for those involved in it acknowledges the congregation's awareness of the need for the presence and work of the Holy Spirit in their worship. Prayers for worship services are typically both intercessions on behalf of everyone involved and times for practicing openness to the guidance of the Holy Spirit.

E X A M P L E S

The most common form of shared prayer for the worship services of a congregation is the "prayer with the choir" led by the pastor just before all enter the sanctuary. An expansion of this format includes laypeople who are not in leadership roles in the service. They join the pastor and other worship leaders before the service to pray with and for them.

Laypeople join the ministers and lay worship leaders twenty minutes before the first of two Sunday morning services in Dee Hazen's church. For fifteen minutes they pray spontaneously for everything that will be going on at the church during the next three hours—for the worship service and its leaders; for those who worship; for the ushers and greeters; for visitors; for the Sunday school and those who teach and learn there; and for anything else that is happening any given Sunday morning. Five minutes before the service, the preacher for the morning gives a brief statement about what he or she hopes for the sermon for the day and then kneels. The others gather around, lay hands on the preacher, and pray for the message. From this time of prayer they move directly to the service.

A third pattern involves laypersons' praying for a service as it is taking place. They may pray in another location either before or after they have come to worship or during the service as they participate in it.

Charles Mathison's church schedules a prayer time each week from 4:00 to 5:00 on Saturday afternoon for people to stop by the church and pray for the worship services and the Sunday-school classes on the following day. A prayer guide gives information about the worship leaders, preachers, and musicians for the next day's services as well as suggestions of other persons or groups in need of prayer. Most of the people who participate stay for the full hour, praying quietly for the concerns listed in the prayer guide for which they feel called to pray.

Voices of Experience

❖ Information about the content of the worship service, the names of those who will be leading, and any special emphases for the day help people who are praying to focus the prayers and to be specific.

❖ Newcomers will appreciate a list of people for whom to pray. Include not only the pastor and liturgist for the day but musicians, acolytes, ushers, greeters, parking lot hosts, visitors, Sunday-school teachers, Sunday-school class members, coffee hour hosts, people who come to church with special needs on a given day. All can be lifted up in prayer. Keep the list current with suggestions about needs for special occasions.

❖ The period just before a service is important for pastors and other worship leaders. Anyone who prays with them at this time has a sacred trust and should be affirming and supportive. This is not the time to discuss other business with the pastor. In these moments, let all prepare their hearts and minds for the task of leading people in worship.

8 Telephone Prayer Ministry

Clark looked up from his reading to the wall clock. It's 10:30 and time to go to bed, he realized. So he moved from his chair to the desk and picked up the telephone. As the first step in his bedtime routine, he dialed the number of the church's voice mailbox reserved for him and dictated the daily devotional for the next day. In his rich baritone voice, he read a passage of scripture, a brief devotional thought on the reading, and a prayer. As he hung up the phone, he noted with satisfaction his log of more than seven hundred passages of scripture on which he had dictated Dial-a-Prayer devotionals in the more than two years he had been on this job. As a retired pastor in his mid-eighties, he had made this his ministry. He regularly received expressions of gratitude from people who often picked up the phone, dialed the well-publicized number, and heard a word from God in Clark's voice. Just recently Clark had expanded this ministry by sending the day's prayer requests by e-mail to a list of thirty people who checked in with him at their computers.

Fran Fletcher picked up her telephone and called the Prayer Request Line voice mailbox at her church. She heard first her own voice welcoming callers and inviting

99

them to leave their prayer requests. The publicly available number was used frequently. Fran keyed in the private code available only to the prayer team for retrieving messages in the voice mailbox. As part of her routine at the end of the day, she checked in to hear prayer requests and to include these requests in her bedtime prayers. Tonight she listened to three requests, wrote them down in her prayer record book, and began her prayer time. As coordinator for this crisis prayer ministry, she checked the mailbox regularly to erase outdated messages or messages that others would already have recorded in their notebooks. She alone used the code to erase. Although the requests were erased to make space in the voice mailbox, the needs were still in the prayers of the team. The system made it possible for members of the prayer team to retrieve prayer requests at their convenience.

John would be sitting in the hospital for a long time on Thursday. His wife, Edith, was scheduled for a difficult and lengthy surgery. The hospital was an hour's drive from their home, and many of their friends would be at work on that day. So the church gave John a pager with a vibrator signal to take with him for his long vigil. Members of the church took the telephone number of the pager. During the day, when they thought of John and Edith, they dialed the pager number and then paused to pray for their friends in the hospital. John felt the pager vibrate repeatedly during the day and knew that many prayers surrounded him and Edith, as he sat alone and waited.

George sat alone in the telephone prayer ministry room of his church. He was working a two-hour shift tonight on the prayer-request line his large urban church provided for the community. The phone was not ringing, but George was praying. He had a list of the requests received earlier, and he joined those who had answered these calls in praying for the people who had called. He also spent time in prayer for the ministries of his church. It was a quiet night, so George had time to pray for guidance in dealing with a difficult situation at work. Suddenly the phone rang. George answered and spent the next fifteen minutes talking and praying with a man who identified himself as Harry. That afternoon Harry had learned from his doctor that he had cancer. He was divorced and lived alone, and as night had fallen, his loneliness had become oppressive. He reached out for someone who could be with him in his anxiety and distress. George listened with compassion to facts and feelings, asking gentle questions to help Harry share his story. He asked for Harry's specific request for prayer and then prayed for the distraught man as he listened. After the prayer, George asked Harry if there were any other way the church could be helpful to him and invited him to come to the worship service on Sunday. Immediately after the call, George wrote Harry's name and prayer need on a list for others to lift in prayer later.

Kathy was dreading tomorrow. She had come halfway across the country to attend the trial of her brother, charged with drunk driving in an accident that left a young woman seriously injured. The evidence against him seemed overwhelming. As Kathy prepared for bed, the motel room telephone rang. Her pastor was on the line. After catching up on Kathy's news, he prayed with her for her brother and his family, for the injured young woman and her family, for all the people who would be involved in the trial, and for Kathy in her pain. Together they prayed the Lord's Prayer and said amen.

The telephone has been around long enough for Christians to figure out a lot of creative ways to use this technology to pray with and for one another. Still some people are surprised to discover that one does not have to be physically present to be able to pray with another person. The telephone can carry the words of a prayer to the heart of someone on the other end of the line quite effectively.

E X A M P L E S

Dial-a-Prayer represents one of the earliest uses of the telephone for prayer ministry. Although it has been the subject of jokes and cartoons over the years, the concept continues to serve well as a way to reach out for another human voice in prayer in time of need. Today voice mailboxes can be used to gather prayer requests and to make those requests available to people dedicated to offering intercessory prayer.

Prayer-request hot lines are best suited to large churches or cooperative community organizations because they require a large number of personnel to assure access for long hours. Some churches supplement an on-site telephone prayer center by using call forwarding during the hours that are difficult to staff. At closing time, the telephone number to which calls are transferred is dialed in.

Linelle Kelley's rural congregation operates a small-church version of the prayer-request hot line. Members who are willing to pray with people over the telephone receive calls at their homes as needed. The congregation of eighty in a town of 150 people has created an effective prayer ministry with nothing more than word-of-mouth publicity. In a medium-sized church, staff in the office could channel prayer requests to members of the prayer team, who then promptly respond to the callers.

Terry Teykl reports on a church in Valdosta, Georgia, that uses a cell phone for a crisis ministry. Volunteers carry the cell phone for designated periods of time, ensuring that the phone can be answered twenty-four hours a day without confining a volunteer to a specific location. The cell phone number, printed on magnets, has been placed in strategic locations around the community, inviting people to call for prayer. "Imagine," Teykl says, "what it would be like to be standing by the pay phone at the hospital, ready to call the family to report bad news, when you see a number to call for prayer to help you find strength and hope."[17]

The telephone prayer chain, with all its various adaptations, also uses this medium to link people together in prayer. See chapter 2 for a discussion of prayer chains.

The Upper Room Living Prayer Center operates twenty-four hours a day, seven days a week. Volunteers receive prayer requests by telephone and pray with those who call. After each call, a volunteer forwards the prayer request to one of 350 Upper Room Covenant Prayer Groups located all over the world. Members of the selected group pray for the request for thirty days. The center receives more than 20,000 prayer requests each month. Prayer requests are received at the center's telephone number: 1-800-251-2468.

Any group of two or more persons in a local church can be chartered as an Upper Room Covenant Prayer Group by following these steps: (1) Complete a six-session study of the basic manual (*The Workbook of Living Prayer* by Maxie Dunnam); (2) obtain a pastor's approval; (3) choose a group name; and (4) designate one person to receive the prayer requests by mail.

The groups covenant to meet at least once a month for study and prayer. Many groups meet more often, every two weeks or weekly. Members agree to pray for specific needs in the local community as well as requests coming from The Upper Room Center.

The Upper Room Prayer Center staff provide chartered groups with recommendations for study resources. These resources offer members direction and guidance in prayer while they are actively connected with a wide community of intercession.

A local church Covenant Prayer Group may sign up to serve as a Remote Prayer Center. Phone calls that come in to The Upper Room Prayer Center in Nashville can be automatically transferred to a church or home for an assigned period of time. The local group commits to staff the phone with two volunteers during the assigned time period, to pray with those who call, and to refer callers' requests to the network of Covenant Prayer Groups through The Upper Room Prayer Center. The long-distance costs of the transfer from Nashville are paid by the local group. Additional training resources for this ministry are provided by The Upper Room Prayer Center.

Some local churches list in their bulletins, newsletter, or on their Web sites the telephone number for The Upper Room Living Prayer Center as a way of providing a telephone prayer ministry to their members and community.

V O I C E S   O F   E X P E R I E N C E

Terry Teykl gives the following guidance to those who operate a church telephone prayer ministry:

❖ Choose carefully when commissioning persons to answer calls in a telephone prayer ministry. Look for individuals who are mature, stable, compassionate Christians, good listeners who believe that God is a good listener and answers prayer.

❖ A telephone prayer ministry is intended for prayer, not for telephone counseling. When training people to receive calls, caution against giving advice to callers.

❖ Take precautions to protect those who receive calls. Instruct them not to give out their name or location to callers. Facilities used for prayer centers need to be well lighted. Some centers use a combination lock on the door, and the combination is known only to those who come to pray. Also instruct those receiving calls not to share telephone numbers of church staff. If a staff person is needed in a situation, let the staff person return the call.

❖ Make a list of emergency and referral telephone numbers from the community available to those who answer calls.

❖ Because a ringing telephone may distract from prayer, consider separating the space for answering calls from the space where people come to pray.

❖ When a telephone number is made available for prayer requests, everyone who has access to that phone needs to prepare to answer appropriately and to handle all calls.

❖ It is usually necessary to train people for praying with others on the telephone. Modeling by a leader is helpful.[18]

9 Internet Prayer Ministry

On the poster you see the face of a woman looking at a computer monitor screen. Under the picture are the words "All work and no pray? Give yourself some space. Take ten minutes and pray online with Sacred Space. www.sacredspace.ie." A second poster simply depicts a laptop computer identified as "PRAYSTATION." Under the picture is this assurance: "Yes, you can pray at your computer, and here's how. www.sacredspace.ie." A third poster shows two computer Internet icons—STOP and REFRESH—followed by this message: "Stop and refresh yourself at Sacred Space."

Available to download and print from the site, these posters advertise a Web site provided by the Irish Jesuits from their media center in Dublin, Ireland. The site is updated daily with a new passage of scripture and provides guidance through a session of prayer in six stages.

Praying together has moved into cyberspace. Christians are now shifting many of their centuries-old ways of praying together easily and naturally into the communication channels of the Internet. As technology develops, prayer sites will be adapted, and people will put new equipment to use for connecting and praying together. This chapter will need constant updating!

E X A M P L E S

One of the simplest uses of cyberspace technology is the e-mail prayer chain. A prayer request is sent out to a list of people who have agreed to the guidelines of prayer-chain participation. When they check their e-mail, they find the request. Updates about the situation surrounding the request can be distributed the same way, so that prayers may evolve as circumstances change. Terry L. Meyer reports that some people give both their work and home e-mail addresses to the operators of the prayer chain to avoid delays in getting messages.

Fran Boyer, Webmaster for a local church, feels that networking via e-mail is bringing caring back into a congregation that has changed due to growth in recent years. The church employs e-mail to communicate concerns with its ever-increasing number of members. Members receive updates on people's health issues and reminders about surgeries or medical procedures, enabling them to keep particular individuals in their prayers. Prayer lists are compiled for different groups, such as Sunday-school classes and men's and women's organizations.

Chatroom technology makes virtual group gatherings possible. Laura Sappington's Emmaus reunion group meets online weekly at 8:00 P.M. on Monday nights using MSN Messenger Service. The meeting of the spiritual-growth group begins with a list of prayer concerns followed by silent prayer. Using the Emmaus reunion group accountability checklist, members discuss what they have accomplished for Christ during the week. The meeting usually lasts between one and two hours, depending on the number of participating members, who have become an extended family and support group for one another. Members appreciate the advantage of remaining in their own homes with their families while still communicating with the group. "If anything comes up while I am online," Laura says, "I can just attend to that situation and still be involved in the discussion." One disadvantage is that members do not meet one another face-to-face.

Some denominational headquarters use their Web sites to facilitate praying together among the churches of the denomination. The United Church of Christ provides a Calendar of Prayer to keep local congregations in touch with people around the world who are serving in Christ's name. Current stories about their ministries provide content for prayers on their behalf. The calendar's format ensures ease in printing out each week's intercessions for the

Sunday bulletin of the local churches. United Church of Christ members can find a prayer for the current day on page one of the denomination's Web site. The introduction there notes: "By joining hands with UCC members throughout the country in prayer, we honor our covenant to each other and remember that God has baptized us into a body that extends through space and time" (www.ucc.org/worship/calender).

The Evangelical Lutheran Church in America offers "prayer ventures" through automatic e-mail. Prayers that focus on ELCA missionaries and global mission concerns as well as on new congregations, pastors, and outreach ministries in the United States and the Caribbean are delivered daily via a "Read Only" mailing list (www.elca.org/it/list/list-pv.html). Daily Bible reading selections appear on the Web site or may be received by automatic e-mail delivery.

The Upper Room Web site, found at www.upperroom.org, presents several opportunities for inspirational reading as well as information and online conversation about spiritual formation. A daily devotional reading, including scripture and a brief prayer is offered.

The Sacred Space Web site of the Irish Jesuits in Dublin, Ireland, designed for individuals at their separate computers, makes it possible for thousands of people around the world to pray the same scriptures following the same format on the same day. The creators think of their visitors as praying together. Emanating from the Jesuit Communication Center in Dublin, Sacred Space offers an order of prayer based on the writings of Saint Ignatius and of contemporary Jesuit writers, centered on the meditative reading of a passage of scripture for the day. The Web site invites the visitor to "make a sacred space in your day, and spend ten minutes, praying here and now, as you sit at your computer, with the help of on-screen guidance and scripture chosen specially for every day." Available for viewing one step at a time, the prayer order includes six steps. The prayer guidance for each of these steps changes periodically, but here is a sample of each:

1. The Presence of God:

I pause for a moment
and remember that all is a gift,
flowing, in each moment, from the hands of a
loving God.
The Giver is always with me, even now,
attentive to me.

2. Freedom:

I ask for the grace to believe
in what I could be and do
if only I allowed God, my loving Creator,
to continue to create me, guide me, and shape me.

3. Consciousness:

How do I find myself today? Where am I with God?
   Do I have something to be grateful for?
         Then I give thanks.
      Is there something I am sorry for?
         Then I ask for forgiveness.

4. The Word:

This reminder precedes a scripture passage for the day: *I read the Word of God slowly, a few times over, and I listen to what God is saying to me.* This question follows the passage: *What are you saying to me, Lord?*

5. Conversation:

      What is stirring in me as I pray?
      Am I consoled, troubled, left cold?
      I imagine Jesus himself standing or
            sitting at my side
      And I share my feelings with him.

6. Conclusion:

      Glory be to the Father, and to the Son,
            and to the Holy Spirit
      As it was in the beginning, is now and
            ever shall be
      World without end. Amen.[19]

Each separate page offers one step in the prayer followed by two options—"Prayer Guide" or "Move On." Newcomers to the site can find guidance or instruction on how to pray by clicking on "Prayer Guide" at each step. Detailed suggestions on such subjects as body, breathing, and listening exercises to help one become aware of the presence of God and instructions on how to do an examination of consciousness, how to read scripture meditatively, or how to converse with Jesus are included in these guides. When each step in prayer is completed, one goes to the next step by clicking "Move On." A click on the benediction "Amen" brings up an end page with connections to other information, links, and an opportunity to register or read feedback.

The process may sound complicated, but it moves smoothly. A newcomer to the site very quickly begins to feel at home. The uncluttered format facilitates concentration on praying.

VOICES OF EXPERIENCE

A major concern for all Internet activities is the protection of privacy. A *Wall Street Journal* reporter addressed this subject under the headline "Internet sites leave some praying for privacy" (carried in the Sunday, March 11, 2001, Orange County *Register*). Special concern was raised about requests for prayer describing personal information that might be of an embarrassing nature. On some cyber prayer chains reporter Barbara Carton found full names attached to requests. The reporter followed up and found that these persons had not given permission for this information to be put on the World Wide Web.

When information on one site is passed on to other prayer chains, retrieving or correcting it often becomes impossible. Months later an outdated, embarrassing, or inaccurate prayer request may still be floating around out there in cyberspace. Acknowledging such risks, The Upper Room Web site provides an opportunity for people to request prayers for others, but subsequently the requests are edited to remove any information that would identify the person or situation needing prayer before the request is given to Covenant Prayer Groups.

10 Prayer Retreat

"Except for the loud snoring in the cabins at night, the men's retreat last weekend was a wonderful experience," Edward Martin reported to the congregation on Sunday morning. Twenty-six men had spent two nights at a church-owned camp, sharing rustic cabins, cooking their meals together, laughing and talking and praying together. The fellowship had been warm, the meals good, the music memorable, and the presentation and prayer times richly meaningful. Some of the men attended the retreat every year, remembered it with pleasure, and looked forward to "next time." For others this retreat had been a first-time experience approached with some trepidation. They were not sure about either "retreating" or spending so much time praying. But other guys they liked and respected thought it was a good idea, so they had tried it. The fact that their pastor led the retreat had helped too. The weekend had been a pleasant surprise for the newcomers, and everyone had welcomed talking at length about faith and life with other Christian men and praying together without feeling pressured by time.

A retreat setting provides time for a more leisurely experience with prayer than is possible in shorter-term sessions. The sense of community that can develop in a group on retreat fosters support, strength, and encouragement for all. Relationships among persons on the retreat and between each person and God can deepen in a time set aside from the noise and busyness of ordinary life simply to be present to God with one another.

The Bible gives us some powerful examples of individual "prayer retreats." Jacob spent the night in a lonely place beside the road as he made a journey. He stopped at sunset and as he rested in the quiet, he heard God speak to him with promises and assurance for the future. Among other things, he heard God say, "Know that I am with you and will keep you wherever you go." Jacob responded in awe: "Surely the Lord is in this place." Jacob was a changed man after this experience, leaving that time and place with commitment: "The LORD shall be my God" (Gen. 28:10-22). Moses went off to a mountain for his prayer retreat. During his time "apart" he heard the voice of God giving guidance that would shape the lives of the Hebrews as they moved into their promised land (Exod. 19–20). Jesus frequently took time to retreat for prayer. He began his ministry with a retreat of forty days in the wilderness where he sorted out the direction for his life. On one occasion he took Peter, James, and John to a mountain where they witnessed Jesus' transfiguration and heard the voice of God speaking to them: "This is my Son, the Beloved; with him I am well pleased; listen to him!" (Matt. 17:1-13).

Uninterrupted time for reflection and prayer characterizes most contemporary prayer retreats. On "silent retreats," printed resources guide participants' reading and reflection, and the opportunity for conversation with a spiritual director may be offered. Most group prayer retreats, however, include speakers, small-group discussion, and informal group fellowship. Corporate worship and recreation frequently occupy part of the schedule. Whatever the format or location, a retreat provides a setting where people can leave their daily routines and focus their attention on their relationship with God.

E X A M P L E S

In his book *Spiritual Life in the Congregation: A Guide for Retreats*, Rueben Job offers the following outline for a churchwide retreat based on the theme "Come Away and Rest—A Time Apart."

Day One

3:00–5:00	Gathering/Registration/Getting Settled
5:30	Evening Meal

6:15	Welcome and Announcements
6:30	Worship/Prayer
	Theme: *Come Aside and Rest*
	Scripture: Mark 6:30-32
7:00	Presentation/Activity
	Theme: *Chosen*
	Scripture: Ephesians 1; Isaiah 42:1-4; John 15:12-17
	Lecture/Sermon on the Theme (20 minutes)
	Questions for Small Groups and Plenary on the Theme:

- Have you ever felt "chosen"? Describe how it felt.
- How are we "chosen in Christ"?
- What does it mean to you to be "chosen in Christ"?

	Small Groups (50 minutes)
	Plenary (20 minutes)
8:30	Fellowship/Recreation/Snacks
9:30	Night Prayers
10:15	Rest, Reading, and Reflection

Day Two

7:30	Personal/Family Prayer and Reflection/Nature Walk/Exercise
8:00	Breakfast
9:00	Morning Prayers
9:30	Presentation/Activity
	Theme: *Called*

Scripture: Isaiah 42:6-9; Romans 1:1-7; John 10:1-10

Lecture/Sermon (20 minutes)

Questions for Personal Reflection; Small Groups; and Plenary Discussion:

- What do you think of when you hear the word *called*?
- How have you felt called during your life?
- How do you think God is calling today?

Personal Reflection (40 minutes)

10:30	Break
11:00	Small Groups (20 minutes)
	Plenary (40 minutes)
11:45–1:00	Lunch
1:00–2:00	Silence/Rest
2:00	Presentation/Activity

    Theme: *Sent*

    Scripture: Exodus 3:7-12; Isaiah 6:1-8; John 1:6-8; Luke 9:1-16

Questions for Personal, Small Group, and Plenary Reflection:

- Can you think of anyone who you believe was sent by God?
- What are the characteristics of those sent by God?
- How are we being sent today?
- What can our congregation do

to become more obedient to God's sending?

Lecture/Sermon (20 minutes)

Small Groups (45 minutes)

3:00	Break
3:30	Plenary Discussion
4:15	Free Time until Dinner
5:30	Dinner
7:00	Talent Show, Movie, or All-Church Recreation, Games, Nature Walk, etc.
9:00	Snacks
9:45	Evening Prayers
10:30	Rest/Reading

Day Three

7:30	Personal/Family Prayer and Reflection/Nature Walk/Exercise
8:00	Breakfast
9:00	Morning Prayers
9:30	Presentation/Activity

Theme: *Sustained*

Scripture: Exodus 16:1-21; Psalm 127:1-2; Matthew 15:32-39

Questions for Personal, Small Group, and Plenary Reflection:

• What is your greatest need?

• How would you like God to provide?

- What can you do to help answer your prayer?
- What is the greatest need of your church?
- What can you do to answer that need?

Lecture/Sermon (20 minutes)
Small Groups (20 minutes)
Plenary (20 minutes)

10:00 Break
10:30 Closing Worship/Eucharist
      Theme: *Twelve Baskets Full*
      Scripture: Matthew 14:13-21
12:00 Lunch (include time for evaluation/witness)[20]

This design assumes that childcare will be provided for toddlers and babies and that older children and young people will be participating in activities appropriate to their age. Plans for a Youth Retreat, an Older Adult Retreat, a Personally Guided Retreat, a Private Retreat, and an Action Retreat are also outlined in Job's book.

A design for a group prayer retreat with an emphasis on learning to pray is available in the combination of two books, *Responding to God: A Guide to Daily Prayer* and the *Leader's Guide* for that book. Using resource material from the basic text, the *Leader's Guide* outlines plans for a retreat on the theme "Weaving Prayer into the

Tapestry of Life," combining group study of prayer with time for practicing prayer.

VOICES OF EXPERIENCE

❖ If possible, hold a retreat in an out-of-the-way place, protected from the distractions of the telephone and of people's coming and going.

❖ Plan for meals to be prepared and served by persons who are not involved in the retreat.

❖ Ask retreatants to plan to stay for the full time if possible.

❖ The best time frame for a retreat includes a minimum of two nights, but brief retreats of even a half day can be worthwhile. The longer format gives time for people to settle in, for community to develop, and for a leisurely schedule that includes music, worship, recreation, and relaxation.

❖ Let the schedule include time for people to relax and to unwind from periods of engagement and to digest the content of the sessions. Resist the temptation to pack the schedule too full.

❖ Music can add an important dimension to a prayer retreat. Singing the prayers of the church touches the heart and spirit and moves the retreat experience to a deeper level. Quality song leadership and instrumental accompaniment are important to an effective music program.

❖ Be sure a retreat is on the church calendar early—at least six months ahead of the date—so people have time to plan to attend.

11 Prayer Breakfast

Rhea Zakich was there when the doors of the restaurant opened for breakfast. Prayer-breakfast people had been the first customers on Thursday mornings for more than thirteen years. Beginning at 6:00 A.M., the prayer-breakfast group adjourned promptly at 7:00 A.M. Upon arriving, the participants moved quickly to their regular back room, sat at tables of four, and began with ten minutes of singing accompanied by guitar. During the singing the waitress who served them every week and knew the routine took breakfast orders. Rhea, the prayer group's leader, had arranged a special menu and payment plan for the group with the restaurant owner. The customers placed the correct amount of money in a cup on the table, and at the end of the session, one person collected the cups and took care of the bill and the tip. The singing was followed by a fifteen-minute "lesson." Having begun as a Lenten study group, members had continued the pattern of having an informational or inspirational message. The food was delivered as group members began "table talk" time when they responded for fifteen minutes to the lesson. Usually discussion questions were provided, with the understanding that "table talk" offered time for "marveling at each person's unique experience—no teaching or preaching, just listening." The last fifteen minutes included large-group discussion and prayer. Everyone attending would be prayed for during the breakfast time. Sometimes the participants prayed at the tables first, but during the last few minutes the whole group always joined hands in a circle for group prayer.

Preston Price had received an invitation to the President's Prayer Breakfast in Washington, D.C. The member of the House of Representatives from his district had arranged the invitation for him, so he flew to Washington for a day of faith community activities that began with the annual President's Prayer Breakfast. The gathering was intended to be an egalitarian fellowship of people of faith concerned about the life of the nation. Name tags for the large crowd of attendees were simple, just each person's first and last name and hometown. Guests took their seats wherever they liked at the tables, and there was no head table. Only three dignitaries, visiting heads of state, were introduced. Preston saw similarities to other civic prayer breakfasts he had attended—the mayor's prayer breakfast in one town and a community prayer breakfast organized by the ministerial association in another town. People of diverse faith traditions had come together to affirm the unity of their concerns for their common community and to pray together for that community. As the featured speaker at the Washington prayer breakfast, the President talked about the importance of his faith in his life and work and shared in the prayer.

A prayer breakfast is simply a prayer meeting in the morning with a shared breakfast meal. It may be a one-time event, an annual occasion, a monthly meeting, or a weekly sharing time. The combination of good fellowship and an opportunity to pray together makes the prayer breakfast attractive. Large groups and small groups can use this format. The format can be simple for a small group—visit, eat breakfast, share in prayer, and go to work. For a large group the program can be expanded to include music, guest speakers, Bible study, faith sharing, and focused prayer for special occasions.

The prayer breakfast works well as a community or ecumenical event. For a larger event, attention may be centered on the message of the speaker or speakers and on prayers led by community leaders. If people at the breakfast are used to praying aloud and they share a style of prayer, the large assembly may form into small groups to pray together. Guided silent prayer is an alternative that involves everyone in prayer.

A mayor's prayer breakfast or community prayer breakfast brings together people of all faiths in a community. Emphasizing fellowship across faith lines, the program is designed to express sensitivity to the faith traditions and the ethnic diversity of all who are involved.

E X A M P L E S

Priscilla Van Giesen's church announced in its newsletter, "Day of Prayer Kicks Off School Year." "The pencils are sharpened, backpacks filled, and first-day outfits chosen, as parents throughout the city prepare to send their children off to begin another school year," the article began. "What better way to begin the year than by surrounding our children and the adults who guide and teach them with our prayers?" A back-to-school prayer breakfast was scheduled for Wednesday of the week after the first day of school, giving everybody a chance to catch their breath after the hectic first day. This time of prayer and praise would include a continental breakfast in the narthex at 9:30 A.M., followed by a time of singing and prayer in the sanctuary. The church invited people who needed to go to work early to stop by between 6:30 and 8:00 A.M. to pray in the sanctuary. A prayer guide would be available, along with coffee and doughnuts. "Reservations are appreciated but not required," concluded the article. There would be no charge for the food but donations would be appreciated. Childcare would be provided for preschoolers with a reservation. Church members were encouraged to invite their neighbors and friends, as the Prayer Breakfast would be open to the entire community.

Early risers who came to the Church of the Resurrection before 8:00 A.M. found a printed prayer guide that suggested praying for students, teachers and support staff, administrators, and local church preschool teachers. The following prayer was included.

Gracious and loving God,
This is a time of excitement and anxiety,
a time of great expectations and uncertainties,
and a time for new beginnings and hopes.
We have come together as a community of
Christians to pray for this new school year.
We want to surround our children and youth
with your love
and support the teachers and helpers who
spend time with each child.
We thank you, Lord, for all the possibilities
this year can hold,
for the wonder and delight of each learner,
and for the time and commitment of those
who teach.
In Jesus' name we pray. Amen.

Those who came later joined in a service of
scripture, singing, and prayer in the sanctuary,
which followed this order of service:

Back-to-School Prayer Service

Welcome
Opening Prayer
For Children
     Hymn: "All in All"
     1 Samuel 1:26-28
     Prayer
For Youth
     Hymn: "Shout to the Lord"
     Philippians 2:14-15

Prayer
For Parents
Hymn: "Happy the Home"
Deuteronomy 6:4-9
Prayer
For Teachers, Administrators, and Staff
Hymn: "Spirit of the Living God"
James 3:13-18
Prayer
For Our Community
Hymn: "Seek Ye First"
Philippians 4:4-9
Prayer
Closing

The following format could work for a large-group or formal prayer breakfast:

- Welcome and introduction of the breakfast leadership team
- Table grace
- Breakfast, during which music may be played
- Special music
- A message from the speaker on a faith theme of mutual interest
- A general prayer on a predetermined theme or topic of interest to the group
- Benediction

VOICES OF EXPERIENCE

❖ By sticking with a simple menu for breakfast, a group won't let the meal become a distraction from the primary purpose of the meeting. A buffet simplifies the meal logistics for a large group.

❖ If several churches, denominations, or faith groups sponsor the breakfast together, remember to plan the program with sensitivity to the traditions and prayer styles of the various groups.

❖ If tickets are not sold, a basket may be placed at the entrance for donations. An accompanying sign may suggest an amount or simply state, "A contribution to the cost of the breakfast would be appreciated." The Church of the Resurrection invites specific donations in its prayer-breakfast publicity.

❖ Greeters, ushers, hosts, and hostesses can offer hospitality at a community or cooperative event where people may not know one another or be familiar with the facilities or the program.

12 Praying the Scriptures Group

Most churches have at least one Bible-*study* group. Some churches have hundreds of people involved in studying the Bible in Sunday-school classes and weekday groups. But groups that gather to *pray* the scriptures with one another are less common.

Reading the scriptures devotionally is an ancient Christian tradition. Practices that could be described as "praying the scriptures" spring from the deepest roots of our tradition and have many variations. One of the most popular ways to "pray the scriptures" is based on the Rule of Saint Benedict written in the sixth century. This tradition recommends a slow, meditative reading of scripture combined with periods of silent reflection. Time spent with the scriptures was to be an encounter with God in Christ in the midst of daily life. The purpose of reading the Bible went beyond gleaning information. For Benedict, active reading and open listening to scripture in the middle of one's imperfect life brought a gradual transformation into Christlikeness. Bible study was thus prayer with the scriptures. In the twelfth century a systematic delineation of this way of praying outlined four stages: (1) reading (*lectio*), (2) meditation (*meditatio*), (3) prayer (*oratio*), and (4) contemplation (*contemplatio*). In the twelfth century, Guigo II the Carthusian wrote in a book titled *The Ladder of Monks*, "Reading seeks for the sweetness of a blessed life, meditation perceives it, prayer asks for it, contemplation tastes it." This four-stage approach to Bible reading has become known as *lectio divina* (pronounced lex-ee-oh dih-vee-nuh), or divine reading.[21]

Because *lectio divina* was so closely identified with the monastic movement, it fell into disuse during the Reformation (sixteenth century) and then was overshadowed by the rational study of scriptures after the Enlightenment (eighteenth century). Recently, however, new forms of *lectio* are becoming popular among those who want to encounter God through the Word.

Groups praying the scriptures seek spiritual nourishment through encounter with God, experienced by engagement with God's Word in scripture. But the *lectio divina* methodology is not limited to scripture. Other inspirational sources may be used, including life experience, which can be a wellspring for an awareness of God's presence and for dialogue with God's spirit. In a group setting, a specific structure guides the members through the four stages of *lectio divina.* This structure makes it possible for all members of the group to share in the leadership, and professional leadership is not necessary.

Group meetings for praying the scriptures may include or complement other elements. A session may be scheduled just before a regular church committee, staff, or board meeting. Time for praying the scriptures together could be combined with a support group, scheduled to include a shared meal, extended for intercessory prayer, or expanded into time for working on a project. In scheduling, remember that the *lectio divina* process itself normally takes between twenty-five and forty minutes, depending on the size of the group.

The Spiritual Formation Bible: Growing in Intimacy with God through Scripture provides resources for praying the scriptures. Special features in this Bible's format encourage reflective reading and life application of God's redemptive activity in history. *Opening to God: Guided Imagery Meditation on Scripture* by Carolyn Stahl Bohler offers fifty meditations designed to encourage experience of God through scripture-based exercise of the imagination.

E X A M P L E

Norvene Vest's book *Gathered in the Word: Praying the Scripture in Small Groups* outlines the following format for group participation in *lectio divina*. It includes time for reading, talking, silent reflection, and prayer.

The Group *Lectio Divina* Process

After a period of preparation, the leader reads through a short passage from scripture. The leader, having asked the group members to listen attentively for a particular word or phrase that seems to be given them, reads the passage slowly a second time. After a minute of silence, the leader invites each to speak aloud the word or phrase heard and received from the passage.

Then a member other than the leader reads the same passage aloud. In silence the group members ponder how the passage seems to touch their lives. Again at the leader's invitation each briefly speaks aloud his or her sense of being touched.

Another group member reads [the] same passage aloud yet again. In silence the group members reflect on what the passage seems to be inviting them to do or be over the next few days. The leader invites each of the members to speak aloud of their invitation.

Finally each member prays that the person to the right will receive power to do or be as he or she feels called.[22]

Members may choose not to share verbally but to pass for any reason or no reason, or to pray silently when it is their turn to pray.

VOICES OF EXPERIENCE

❖ The best scripture passages for *lectio divina* are brief (no more than ten verses) and active with concrete images. The Gospels and the Psalms are good sources. Passages heavy with doctrine, history, or ritual are much more challenging.

❖ Group size is ideally smaller than ten persons. Five or six is a good number for the process of group *lectio.*

❖ An initial covenant to meet weekly for a minimum of three months will give group members a chance to develop trust and to become comfortable with the process. The reception of new members into an established group will keep the group fresh and lively.

❖ Leadership can be shared in the group.[23]

13 Centering Prayer Group

Ann belongs to a centering prayer group that has been meeting regularly since 1994. It very quickly became ecumenical, one of its great strengths. The group meets every other Sunday night for an hour and a half. The session begins with a brief reading from scripture, twenty minutes of centering prayer in silence, thirty minutes of spiritual formation, followed by thirty minutes of discussion. (The group has used the videotapes by Thomas Keating as a resource for the spiritual-formation segment.) Normal attendance at the group is twelve to fifteen, and new people are welcome to join the group. Ann is pleased that capable and sustained leadership gives strength to the group. Members have developed a strong bond, even though they do not often see one another between meetings.

Ann had been having a hard time sustaining the practice of centering prayer on her own. She was enormously grateful to discover that others were engaging in centering prayer together on a regular basis. The practice of lectio divina *as a complementary discipline has further deepened her relationship with God. When people ask her about centering prayer, she describes it as "a bridge to contemplation"; a method that enhances other prayer forms; a silent prayer beyond words, thoughts, and feelings. In centering prayer Ann feels that she consents to the presence and action of God both during prayer and in daily life. She believes that the practice of centering prayer has allowed her to act more from her true self.*

The popular notion of centering, or contemplative, prayer conjures up one person in solitude and quiet engaged in wordless communion with the spirit of God. To speak of a centering, or contemplative, prayer *group* may then seem a contradiction in terms. But in fact, centering prayer groups do meet as part of the prayer ministry of local churches in order to support, train, and encourage people who want to practice centering prayer.

Centering prayer prepares one to enter into contemplative prayer, where words are not important. Interior silence with openness of heart and mind to the mystery of God's presence and activity is key to this ancient prayer tradition. Contemplative prayer is sometimes described as "resting in God."

In the 1970s three Trappist monks at Saint Joseph's Abbey in Spencer, Massachusetts—William Meninger, Basil Pennington, and Thomas Keating—developed a contemporary adaptation of this ancient way of praying. Keating's book *Open Mind, Open Heart* has become the basic resource for centering prayer. Keating gives four guidelines for centering prayer:

1. Choose a sacred word as the symbol of your intention to consent to God's presence and action within.
2. Sitting comfortably and with eyes closed, settle briefly, and silently introduce the sacred word as the symbol of your consent to God's presence and action within.
3. When you become aware of thoughts, return ever-so-gently to the sacred word.
4. At the end of the prayer period, remain in silence with eyes closed for a couple of minutes.[24]

The sacred word of one or two syllables is to be chosen prayerfully, asking for the Holy Spirit's inspiration in selecting an appropriate word for oneself. Possibilities include *Lord Jesus, Father, Mother, Love, Joy, Peace, Grace, Silence, Faith, Trust, Yes, Kyrie, Shalom.* A simple inward gaze may be used instead of the sacred word.

Keating encourages individuals who practice centering prayer to join a support group. He and the other monks have created a number of books and videotapes designed to encourage the practice of centering prayer. These resources and a series of training workshops and retreats are available through the Contemplative Outreach National/International Office (see Resources for details), as well as materials for learning *lectio divina* as an introduction to contemplative prayer.

E X A M P L E

Judy Lineback organized a centering prayer group in her church about a year after she began the practice on her own. Her group meets from 12:15 to 1:30 P.M., an extended lunch hour, at Christ Church Episcopal, a large downtown parish. In the six years since her group began meeting, two others have sprung from it—a suburban group and an evening group in her city church.

Each gathering works a little differently, but all groups either study a book, watch a video about centering prayer (or a related topic), or practice group *lectio divina;* and all spend time sharing aloud their experiences with centering or contemplative prayer. All conclude their sessions with twenty minutes of centering prayer. Groups who meet for an hour and a half often use the first few minutes for social interaction, getting acquainted with newcomers, and to catch up on news with longtime acquaintances.

V O I C E S   O F   E X P E R I E N C E

❖ Seek out a space for meeting that provides quiet and freedom from interruptions. Place chairs in a circle to facilitate ease of communication. A lighted candle in the center creates an atmosphere for prayer.

❖ Since most groups have both a core membership and a transient membership, plan for a short period at the beginning of each session for getting acquainted or reacquainted.

❖ Encourage regular attendance, which promotes a strong sense of community.

❖ You may time the centering prayer segment by using a tape that begins with meditative music followed by twenty minutes of silence and closes with more music. Thomas Keating suggests that another option for closing is a slow recitation of the Lord's Prayer by the leader while group members listen. Such a closing allows participants "to readjust to the external senses and . . . bring the atmosphere of silence into daily life."[25]

❖ Sharing in discussion time is sharing in faith. Be aware that centering prayer is a heart experience, which does not lend itself to theological or philosophical debate during the sharing period.

14 Prayer in Planning and Decision Making

"A small congregation gathered on a Sunday afternoon to consider its future. The congregation did not face any crises or controversies. There were no emergencies or substantial issues to resolve. The church's life was generally secure. Nevertheless, the pastor, prompted by a vague need to be sure that the church was doing everything 'right,' urged the members to engage in a process of discernment.

"During the discernment process, members recalled stories of their congregation. Many of these stories predated all of the participants. These were the congregation's 'family stories,' passed down at church suppers and around the edges of meetings.

"These family stories revealed that this congregation had always reached out to the community. As the congregation reflected on Scripture, the parable of the great feast in Luke 14:15-24 seemed particularly relevant to their situation. The parable speaks of a dinner to which the host invited a large number of guests. However, after all the guests declined the invitation, the host turned to the community and invited anyone who would come. The parable challenged the congregation to search out people in their community who were not a part of the

church's life. After a time of prayer and silent reflection, participants identified the teens in the community as a group largely missing from the congregation. Following extended conversation, participants began drawing up plans for a youth ministry in their small community, including plans for the use of a building that could house such a ministry.

"None of the people who gathered on that Sunday afternoon could have imagined that they would be led into an intentional ministry with youth. They perceived the life of their congregation as generally complete and satisfying. Only when they opened themselves to the heart of God through their stories, Scripture, prayer, and holy conversation did God's dream for them begin to take shape."[26]

Planning and decision making in the life of the church are appropriately set in the context of prayer. The example of the early church reveals a sense of dependence on the Holy Spirit in making decisions. The first chapter of Acts recounts the disciples' first decision after the ascension of Jesus. They gather to select a successor for Judas. Names are presented— Barsabbas and Matthias. Then the disciples pray, "Lord, you know everyone's heart. Show us which one of these two you have chosen to take the place in this ministry and apostleship from which Judas turned aside . . ." (Acts 1:24-25). In the middle of the agenda, they pray and ask for guidance on a specific decision. Later, when servers are chosen, the disciples bring them forward, lay hands on them, and pray for them (Acts 6:1-7). Still later, when reporting a decision about church policy, the leaders of the church say, "For it has seemed good to the Holy Spirit and to us" (Acts 15:28).

The standard opening prayer of church committee and board meetings acknowledges that the group is gathered to do God's business. God's presence is affirmed and God's guidance is invited in the prayer. The closing prayer—also a common agenda item—gives thanks for God's gifts, commits decisions made and actions taken to God's keeping, and lifts shared concerns in common intercession. These prayers in church business meetings often represent a perfunctory "nod to God," "bookend prayers" that participants scarcely notice. But settings where "two or three" or more have come together in Christ's name to plan and make decisions about the life and work of the church offer an opportunity for rich and meaningful prayer together.

Charles M. Olsen, who has worked extensively at integrating spirituality and administration in the life of the church, suggests a culinary metaphor for prayer. "Prayer," he says, "can be the marinade for the meat of the agenda, rather than the icing on the cake."[27] Olsen's interest in this arena of church life began as concern about burnout among leaders who leave active church involvement after faithfully serving on boards and committees. Instead of finding spiritual growth and enrichment in working with others to plan and make decisions for the work of the church, many people were drained and disappointed. They had approached their work with expectations of something unique and had found church boards to be like administrative groups anywhere. Olsen responded by focusing attention on ways to incorporate prayer as a dimension of the whole meeting in order to open the process to the leading of the Holy Spirit through discernment.

EXAMPLES

Churches responding to the research for this book reported two ways of praying together while planning and making decisions. The first is a style deemed appropriate for business meetings operating under *Robert's Rules of Order*. These meetings can be formal, conforming strictly to the rules, or relaxed and casual. The second way of incorporating prayer in the business of the church follows the process of discernment.

Most church meetings for planning and decision making operate on the democratic principle of majority rule. Participants make motions or suggestions, discuss, and take a vote. The decision is made. Charles Olsen, in his book *Transforming Church Boards into Communities of Spiritual Leaders,* suggests ways to incorporate prayer in appropriate places all through such an agenda.

For example, a member of the group might be prepared to lead the group in an opening prayer specific to the agenda for the meeting. A response of thanksgiving or praise could follow each report. A litany of praise or thanksgiving can follow a special report at the end of a significant event. A moment of prayer could conclude a report on a new ministry to be undertaken. Following discussion on an important issue or decision, a period of silent prayer might give members of the group time to reflect on and pray about their decision before voting. Allowing for such reflection is particularly helpful when conflict or tension has surrounded a discussion or when a decision carries major import. Persons who have been appointed to serve as "gleaners" of ideas while the meeting is in progress can lead the closing prayer, highlighting items for thanksgiving, intercession, petition, and praise, and committing the business transacted to God.

Some groups, Olsen reports, find that lighting a candle at the beginning of a meeting and extinguishing it at the conclusion heighten the expectation that the church's business is God's business and point to the presence of Christ in the midst of deliberations. The inspirational words and music of many prayer hymns and choruses can lift the prayers in the hearts of group members. Hymnbooks and instrumental accompaniment enhances the singing of these prayers.[28]

As an alternative to the usual business-meeting format for church groups, Charles Olsen and Danny Morris have developed resources for a contemporary version of the discernment process. Described in their book *Discerning God's Will Together: A Spiritual Practice for the Church*, this process has roots in both the Quaker consensus model and in the spiritual exercises of Saint Ignatius, among other traditions. The process design facilitates cooperative listening for God's leading. In a meeting where the discernment process is used, the group can deal with all the normal business in the usual way. But extra time is devoted to one item on the agenda because the group feels led to submit this matter to a more thorough process in order to discern the leading of the Holy Spirit. The question then becomes not "What is the will of the majority about this matter?" but "What is the mind of Christ about this?" A decision is made out of dialogue between the human community and the spirit of God and so becomes a prayerful consideration.

From the long tradition of spiritual discernment in the church Morris and Olsen identify ten *movements* that are appropriate for today. They use the term *movements* to avoid the implication that these are steps that must be done in sequence. The process is open and dynamic, flowing back and forth among these movements from beginning to conclusion. These are the movements described by Morris and Olsen:

- *Framing*—identifying the focus for discernment. "A subject for discernment should be clearly stated and agreed upon by the entire group."[29]

- *Grounding* in a guiding principle based on the values, beliefs, and purposes of the group, which may be developed by a leadership team and shared with the group for their refinement and acceptance.

- *Shedding* of ego issues, prejudices, and preconceptions—anything that could block openness to the leading of the Spirit—with the goal of becoming indifferent to all but the will of God.

- *Rooting* in religious and biblical themes, stories, and images that relate to the issue for discernment.

- *Listening* for promptings from the Holy Spirit, for the voices of all who are part of the discerning community and others who will be affected by the decision.

- *Exploring* as many options as possible within the guiding principle.

151

- *Improving* each option until it is the best imaginable.

- *Weighing* the options in response to the leading of God's spirit. Pros and cons may be analyzed, and possible fruits of each option anticipated, followed by reflection on the options in silent prayer or with guided imagery.

- *Closing* with movement toward selection of an option. The group tests for consensus. In the absence of consensus, the group may choose to reach a decision in another way, to make no decision, or to take no action.

- *Resting* "tests the decision by allowing it to rest near the heart to determine whether it brings primarily feelings of consolation (a sense of peace and movement toward God) or desolation (distress and movement away from God)."[30]

V O I C E S   O F   E X P E R I E N C E

❖ A group using the *Robert's Rules of Order* approach may enhance its quality of prayer by asking a worship leader or group to plan and lead worship during meetings. If the worship leader and the group's chairperson work together, various prayer experiences appropriate to the group's agenda can be incorporated.

❖ Limit the number of items submitted to prayerful community discernment to significant decisions that deserve the amount of time and attention involved in the discernment process—no more than one per meeting and perhaps only a few over the period of a year.[31]

❖ Groups may need training in activities that make up the discernment process before they will feel comfortable with it. The process can be introduced a step at a time, with stand-alone opportunities to experience prayer that is primarily listening, to work for consensus on decisions, to tell stories about God's activity in the world, and to remember scriptures that relate to experience.[32]

❖ Initiate the use of discernment in a group with a question that involves little conflict or controversy.[33] Learn the process without the complication of conflict.

❖ Discernment on a major issue may require a longer meeting, a retreat, or several meetings for which everyone can agree to be present and at which only the one agenda item will be considered.

❖ The setting for a meeting using the discernment process is important. A new location may suggest new ways of relating and working together. Ensure that the environment will be quiet and free from distractions and that seating arrangements will allow all group members to see one another easily.

❖ Before the meeting begins, a leadership team should shape the question for discernment by the group.[34]

15 Family Prayer

Bob and Mary had signed up for the new members' class at their church. As the first session began, members of the class introduced themselves, giving a brief personal history and explaining why they were interested in joining the church. When their turn came, Bob and Mary explained together. Their three-year-old daughter had learned to say grace at mealtime in the church's preschool program and had come home insisting that the family have grace before meals. She wanted everyone to hold hands, bow their heads, and say thank you to God before eating. The only problem was that Mommy and Daddy did not know how to pray. So the next Sunday the whole family showed up for church. A few weeks later Bob and Mary were here to make the commitment to membership in the congregation. They were both mildly embarrassed to tell this story yet deeply grateful to the church for the resources and support provided in helping them become a family that every day held hands in a circle and prayed together. This experience with the church had caused unexpected growth for them personally in their own faith and life. The simple custom of praying together before meals had drawn the family closer together and given them a new sense of unity and purpose. "This is a good *direction for us as a family," they agreed, "and we want to build on this foundation."*

A familiar saying states, "The family that prays together stays together." The tradition of praying together in the family comes from deep in our Judeo-Christian heritage. Our Hebrew ancestors in faith included family members of all ages in the rituals of worship. Children were expected to learn the faith in their homes, taught by their parents. Much of what they learned was taught at celebrations of the faith around the family table. Deuteronomy, one of the books of the Law for the Hebrews, includes these instructions:

> Hear, O Israel: The LORD is our God, the Lord alone. You shall love the LORD your God with all your heart, and with all your soul, and with all your might. Keep these words that I am commanding you today in your heart. Recite them to your children and talk about them when you are at home and when you are away, when you lie down and when you rise.
>
> —Deuteronomy 6:4-7

Praying together as a family in the twenty-first century is as important as ever, whether or not children are present. Where children are in the home, contemporary parents often find themselves caught up in busy schedules involving school, work, and community activities with little time for family interaction. Families must deal with a highly stimulating cultural environment that includes powerful and destructive influences for children and young people. Communicating Christian values in this environment is challenging. A pattern of praying together supports the family in finding a common focus and giving direction and purpose to family life. Praying together in a family with children also creates a setting in which children learn to pray themselves by hearing others pray and having the opportunity to share their own prayers. If a family practices this pattern when children are young, the family will find it easier to maintain as everyone matures.

Praying together in families of all ages allows family members to share the bond of faith that strengthens the family ties. Family prayer is a way of affirming common commitments, expressing concerns, and celebrating shared joys. Family prayer time or worship can include the same elements as congregational worship, although usually they are briefer. The family is a small congregation gathered to worship God in prayer.

E X A M P L E S

The most popular times for families to pray together are at mealtimes, at bedtime, in connection with holiday celebrations, and in observance of special family events.

Prayers at mealtime. Praying together as a family can be as simple as sharing in a blessing or grace before meals. Even very young children can learn the ritual of being quiet, bowing heads, closing eyes, and perhaps holding hands while someone speaks words of gratitude and asks for God's blessing on the meal and those who share it. Prayers may be spontaneous or prepared, spoken or sung. Some families have table grace traditions handed down from grandparents; some use a familiar prayer for each meal. Still others include not only words of blessing for the meal but prayers for special interests or concerns of the day.

Families may expand the table grace with a brief daily devotional, incorporating scripture reading, meditation, and a prayer. The prayer may include special concerns of family members, lifting up family members who are not present for blessing, and intercession for others. If a family is part of a church prayer chain, praying for people who have made requests becomes part of that time. (Confidentiality issues would need to be addressed according to the protocol for the chain.) Family members may share in leading mealtime prayer, or one person may assume the task on an ongoing basis. Preschoolers can learn to lead with brief thank-you prayers of their own creation.

Marjorie Thompson, in her book *Family the Forming Center*, describes a pattern for morning prayer used for many years by a family she knows:

> When gathered for breakfast, members share what the coming day holds for them—both what they look forward to and what they are anxious about. Then each family member prays briefly for the others. Not only do family members feel heard, supported, and cared for before leaving home each morning, but they remember one another at critical hours of the day and are eager to find out how things have gone when they gather again for supper.[35]

Bedtime prayers. Children's bedtime presents a natural time for conversation, storytelling, and prayer. Bedtime prayer may be a simple set prayer or a spontaneous prayer rising out of the day's concerns. Shared bedtime prayer provides an opportunity for family members to stay in touch with one another in the midst of busy schedules. A simple format of relating the highs and lows of the day, the joys and concerns, communicates what is going on in the life of each person. Prayers may then reflect what is important in the lives of family members.

Reading Bible stories together at bedtime sets the stage for praying to the God revealed in those stories. Prayers can reflect insights into the nature of God and God's relationship with human beings, as expressed in the scripture read together.

Seasons of the Christian year. Families with children will find the Advent season rich with potential for family worship times. One common practice is lighting Advent candles on a wreath on the Sundays of Advent, adding one candle each week until four candles are lighted on the Sunday before Christmas. Reading scriptures and prayer accompany each candle lighting. All Saints' Day, the first day of November, gives families an opportunity to remember family members who are no longer living, to relate stories about ancestors, and to offer prayers of thanksgiving for their lives. Thanksgiving provides family members of all ages an opportunity to tell one another what they are most thankful for as they gather around the table for the holiday dinner. The blessing for the meal expresses corporate gratitude for all these gifts.

Special events or occasions in the life of a family. Family members are born or adopted, and family members die. They come and go from the family home. Families move into new homes and have anniversaries of special events. Children are baptized, confirmed, graduate. Adults get engaged and married, begin new jobs, retire. At all these major times of transition and change, special prayers or even brief, informal services of worship are both appropriate and pleasing, especially when members of the extended family and friends can be invited to share. Denominational worship resources include prayers and blessings for many such special occasions that families may adapt for their situations.

Many denominations and religious publishing houses produce materials for use in family worship. Several Upper Room resources are appropriate. *The Upper Room* daily devotional guide is useful for all ages with readings brief enough to be read at mealtime. For families with children, *At Home with God: Family Devotions for the School Year* offers daily devotions and activities for September through May. The magazine *Pockets* includes family litanies, articles for parents about children's spirituality, and information on how to use *Pockets* with children. For teenagers, The Upper Room's bimonthly magazine *Devo'Zine* contains daily meditations indexed according to situations teens might face. Teens may choose to share with the family from these devotions.

VOICES OF EXPERIENCE

❖ A local church can help families develop the habit of praying together by

- making appropriate devotional materials available;
- providing occasional workshops for parents on how to pray together as a family. Parents may have questions

161

about how to lead family prayer and be unaware of helpful resources.

- adding to the church library books on family worship and on helping children to learn to pray.

❖ When praying together as a family, use language that everyone involved can understand. The use of everyday conversational tones of voice and language when praying will help everyone feel competent to voice prayers.

❖ With young children, be brief and simple. If a family includes both young children and teenagers, the young children can share and pray first and then be excused from the table, while the teens and parents continue their sharing and praying together.

❖ Develop patterns for regular family prayer so that family members know what to expect and can get into the routine. Establish a time, place, and ritual that will work for everyone. The pattern may need adjustment as the family's life evolves, but having a basic pattern from which to work will ensure the practice becomes an accepted part of family life.

❖ Keep family prayer time positive, hopeful, and cheerful.

16 Covenant Group

The lunch was delicious and the ambience relaxed. As dessert was cleared away, conversation turned to the reason for the meeting. The invitation letter had asked, "Would you like to be part of a clergy support/prayer group that would meet once a month?" The response had been unanimous: "Yes." Now eight people were ready to give shape to the new group. "The pastoral ministry can be isolating and lonely," they agreed. "We need a way to care for and support one another." John had belonged to several groups before, but they had been short-lived and disappointing. After a few meetings, the conversation had centered mostly on church politics. The meetings had been a low priority for the participants and attendance sporadic. This time John was looking for a group experience that would be spiritually nurturing. Sue had also been in several groups over the years. Her past experiences had been valuable, and she missed that support system since her move to a new church.

The ideas began to pour out. Everyone agreed that they wanted a covenant group in the sense of having shared commitments to one another, and they decided on regular, full-time attendance and confidentiality for starters. The agenda took shape by consensus. Each person in turn would share with the group in response to the question from the early Wesley class meetings: "How goes it with your soul?" The time would be divided roughly evenly among members of the group. After each person shared, other group members would take turns praying for that individual before the next person spoke. All agreed that the sharing segments of their meetings would not include advice giving or problem solving, just supportive caring and praying.

Ed offered a room in his centrally located church as a regular place of meeting. The church hostess there would provide light refreshments and coffee. The first Thursday of the month from 8:30 to 10:00 A.M. seemed to suit everyone. At the conclusion of the meeting plans were completed for the birth of a new group. A year later five of the original eight were settled happily into the covenant group and the first-Thursday morning routine of gathering to share their lives and to pray with and for one another.

Covenant groups are distinguished by a commitment the members make. In some groups, members make a commitment to one another. Covenant Discipleship Groups add to that a covenant with God concerning the practice of spiritual disciplines of Christian discipleship, and members hold one another accountable for the practice of these disciplines as defined in agreed-upon terms. Many covenant groups are not prayer groups as such, although praying together is a normal part of each meeting. But the practice of regular prayer is a dimension of Christian discipleship included in such covenants, and group members pray together in the sense of holding one another accountable for and encouraging one another in regular prayer.

E X A M P L E S

Two models that offer the opportunity for spiritual formation through community accountability are Covenant Discipleship Groups, developed by the United Methodist General Board of Discipleship, and the RENOVARÉ program, developed by Richard Foster.

Covenant Discipleship Groups. Based on the model of the Methodist class meetings established in England by John Wesley in the eighteenth century, these groups were popularized in the late twentieth century by the writings of David Lowes Watson. Watson describes the groups: "A covenant discipleship group consists of up to seven people who agree to meet together for one hour per week in order to hold themselves mutually accountable for their discipleship. They do this by affirming a written covenant on which they themselves have agreed."[36] The covenant is adapted from and shaped by the guidelines for Christian living in the world developed by John Wesley in his *General Rules* of 1743. Wesley organized the components of discipleship under two categories: "works of mercy" and "works of piety." Watson

165

defines "works of mercy" as "doing everything possible to serve God and one's neighbor, while avoiding those things that offend God and harm one's neighbor." "Works of piety" involve "doing everything needful to be open to God's grace," such as public worship, the ministries of word and sacrament, private prayer, reading the Bible, and fasting or temperance.[37]

Today's Covenant Discipleship Groups have adapted Wesley's foundations into a more contemporary General Rule of Discipleship: "To witness to Jesus Christ in the world, and to follow his teachings through acts of compassion, justice, worship, and devotion, under the guidance of the Holy Spirit.[38] The specific covenant for each group is developed in the first meeting. Watson's resource materials include a sample covenant that can be adapted by a new group.

A Sample Covenant of Discipleship

Knowing that Jesus Christ died that I might have eternal life, I herewith pledge myself to be his disciple, witnessing to his saving grace, and seeking to follow his teachings under the guidance of the Holy Spirit. I faithfully pledge my time, my skills, my resources, and my strength, to search out God's will for me, and to obey.

I will worship each Sunday unless prevented.

I will receive the sacrament of Holy Communion each week.

I will pray each day, privately, and with my family or with friends.

I will read and study the scriptures each day.

I will return to Christ the first tenth of all I receive.

I will spend four hours each month to further the cause of the disadvantaged in my community.

When I am aware of injustice to others, I will not remain silent.

I will obey the promptings of the Holy Spirit to serve God and my neighbor.

I will heed the warnings of the Holy Spirit not to sin against God and my neighbor.

I will prayerfully care for my body and for the world in which I live.[39]

Weekly meetings are limited to one hour in length. Groups have the flexibility to allow members to remain longer if they want time to visit or work on issues, but the meeting officially closes at the end of one hour. The meeting's agenda is a review of members' accountability to the covenant in the week just past and planning for faithfulness in the days ahead. The group leader asks each member to respond to questions about individual clauses in the covenant, and the members reply to the leader. General group discussion is limited. The leader of the group, in the spirit of Wesley, is to "advise, reprove, comfort or exhort" the members, offering, in Watson's words, "guidance, correction, affirmation, or encouragement."[40] After the first few initial sessions, leadership in the group can rotate, with the leader for the next week chosen at the end of each meeting.

Materials available for covenant discipleship programs for youth and children are listed in Resources.

RENOVARÉ. Richard Foster, author of several best-selling books on spirituality, including *Celebration of Discipline*, describes the development of the RENOVARÉ program of spiritual-formation groups:

> In the fall of 1988, Jim Smith and I started meeting just to see how a nurturing fellowship of mutual accountability might work. I cannot tell you how encouraging and fun-filled those first meetings were: we laughed at our foibles and rejoiced in our successes; we prayed; we made confession; we brought the grace of forgiveness; we made mutual covenants; we challenged and encouraged each other. They were high, holy, hilarious times.[41]

Based on study of many small-group movements, including sixth-century Benedictines, thirteenth-century Franciscans, eighteenth-century Methodists, and twentieth-century Alcoholics Anonymous, Foster and Smith developed a vision and pattern for groups for spiritual growth designed to bring renewal to local churches.

The RENOVARÉ groups are designed to provide balance, knowledge, and mutual encouragement and accountability. Group size varies from two to seven people; meeting time runs from sixty to ninety minutes; leadership rotates among group members. A study guide for the first nine sessions provides a common understanding of the six traditions of Christian faith and witness:

Contemplative (the Prayer-Filled Life)
Holiness (the Virtuous Life)
Charismatic (the Spirit-Empowered Life)
Social Justice (the Compassionate Life)
Evangelical (the Word-Centered Life)
Incarnational (the Sacramental Life)

The meeting agenda includes unison reading of the group covenant and the common disciplines, reports on accountability to the covenant, and plans for the future. The covenant reads, "In utter dependence upon Jesus Christ as my ever-living Savior, Teacher, Lord, and Friend, I will seek continual renewal through Spiritual exercises, Spiritual gifts, Acts of service."[42] The common disciplines are the following:

- By God's grace, I will set aside time regularly for prayer, meditation, and spiritual reading and will seek to practice the presence of God.

169

- By God's grace, I will strive mightily against sin and will do deeds of love and mercy.

- By God's grace, I will welcome the Holy Spirit, exercising the gifts and nurturing the fruit while living in the joy and power of the Spirit.

- By God's grace, I will endeavor to serve others everywhere I can and will work for justice in all human relationships and social structures.

- By God's grace, I will share my faith with others as God leads and will study the Scriptures regularly.

- By God's grace, I will joyfully seek to show forth the presence of God in all that I am, in all that I do, in all that I say.[43]

Meetings conclude with sharing prayer concerns and group prayer.

V O I C E S   O F   E X P E R I E N C E

❖ Confidentiality is essential. Open sharing will occur only when people trust that the information will not go beyond the group.

❖ To encourage a nurturing environment, Richard Foster suggests as a group motto: "Give encouragement as often as possible;

advice, once in a great while; reproof, only when absolutely necessary; and judgment, *never.*"[44]

❖ Invite the involvement of the church pastor and other leaders. More than a courtesy, including these persons and their perspectives integrates the covenant group into the life and work of the congregation.

❖ Provide opportunities for periodic evaluation of the group.

❖ Pilot groups that agree to meet for a year can help with the establishment of a new program of covenant groups in a congregation.

❖ In groups where leadership rotates, the convener plays an important role, since he or she serves as the group's contact with the rest of the congregation and oversees housekeeping matters.

17 Prayer Room or Chapel

Susan Gregg-Schroeder, minister of pastoral care, was aware that the prayer chapel in the New Life Pastoral Counseling Center of her large, urban church was a busy place. No more than eight people could fit comfortably in its small space. Despite its size, the room was quiet and comfortable. It featured a lovely carved oak altar. Counselors in the program encouraged people with whom they met to stop by the chapel for meditation and prayer either before or after counseling sessions. Counselors themselves came to the chapel between sessions or after especially heavy or challenging sessions with clients. The prayer chapel was used regularly by other staff as well.

One young woman developed the habit of spending time in the chapel in connection with each of her counseling appointments. She was struggling with a serious problem, and the counseling continued over an extended time. Occasionally she and the counselor came to the chapel to pray together. As the young woman approached the time when she was ready to end the counseling relationship, she decided that she wanted to be baptized. The healing in her life had been spiritual as well as emotional. An old baptismal font reclaimed from storage stood in the corner of the room and was activated for the occasion.

She was baptized in the community of the church in which her healing had happened and in the small, quiet space that had been church for her.

A room in any church building may be designated the prayer room or prayer chapel and serve as a place where people may pray individually or together. If the room is located near the sanctuary, it can be used after worship services for prayer alone or with intercessors.

Some churches schedule people to be in the prayer room for a block of time each day or each week for constant prayer, while other persons come and go during this period. Some churches schedule specific times for people to come together to pray in the prayer room, such as noon, early morning, or early evening each day. Others simply make the space available for individuals or groups to use for prayer as needed. Churches with crisis telephone ministries often combine the telephone answering center and the prayer room or place the two close together so that call-in requests can be referred easily to persons in the prayer room.

EXAMPLES

Terry Teykl, in his book *Making Room to Pray*, describes a prayer room with prayer stations located around the room, where a person may sit, stand, or kneel while praying. Scripture resources for prayer and prayer requests on the appropriate theme can be posted at each station. Prayer stations may include locations for praising and worshiping God, confessing one's sins, and resting in God's presence, as well as for intercessions. Specific kinds of intercessions can be made at different stations addressing the needs of the world, the nation, the city, the local church, and one's own individual needs. A "crisis" station may be designated for recent or major concerns. One local church designated stations for intercessions for the pastoral staff, missionaries, pregnant women and those with small children, social issues, unsaved friends and neighbors, and church members.

V O I C E S   O F   E X P E R I E N C E

Terry Teykl makes the following suggestions:

❖ Good lighting, heating, and air conditioning are important. If the prayer room is to be used all week, an independent climate control system can keep energy costs down.

❖ Security for those who come to pray should be provided with lights, locks, and access to a telephone for emergency calls.

❖ Plan for handicapped access to the prayer room.

❖ Provide furnishings and equipment of good quality in the room, indicating that the church believes what happens here is important. Maintenance should be carefully monitored.[45]

.

18 Labyrinth Walking

The group gathered quietly in the dimly lighted room and sat in the chairs arranged in a circle around a large square of canvas laid out in the middle of the space. Candles flickered and quiet settled in. In a corner of the room, musicians began to play. A pianist, a violinist, a cellist, and a flautist merged their music into a repeated chant, and the group began to sing. Martha had come into the room with her spirit in turmoil. Her husband was having a bad day with terminal cancer. He had entered a new level of suffering, and the news was not good. Fellowship with the group was like applying a soothing medication on a stinging wound.

The leader stood as the singing ended and began to describe the experience of walking a labyrinth drawn on the canvas. The leader turned to the cellist and asked her, "How do you do it? What is the process for you?" "As I walk into the center," the cellist responded, "I reflect on what I need to let go of in my life. When I step into the center, I wait and listen to hear what messages there are for me. As I walk out, I think about how what I have heard can be integrated into my life." "Do you always hear something when you reach the center?" the leader asked. "Always," the musician responded. "Sometimes I hear more than I can absorb at one time. But there is always insight for me."

The music began again, and group members stood one by one to begin their pilgrimage to the center of the labyrinth. Martha waited and watched. When the time seemed right, she moved to the entrance of the path marked on the canvas and began to walk, reflecting as suggested on what she needed to let go of in her life. Anxiety about her husband's suffering came to mind immediately. The walk became a matter of concentrating on the path and feeling the clarity of emotion in a setting of spiritual serenity. As she reached the center and stepped in, she heard, as clearly as if someone standing next to her had spoken, "Martha, you do not need to carry this load. Bob's dying is between Bob and me. He is my beloved child, and it will be okay. You can let this go." Suddenly the load was gone. Trust and hope and joy took its place. As she walked the path back out of the labyrinth, Martha let this new experience sink in and felt relaxation pour through her body as grace was received and transformed into overflowing gratitude.

The labyrinth looks like a circular maze. But a maze is designed to confuse, with dead ends along the path and a devious design. The labyrinth's design guides the walker on his or her way. A single narrow path opens from the outside of the circle and winds its way into an open space at the middle of the circle. For many, walking the labyrinth provides a unifying experience within and with God. In the open spirit of the meditative walk, the soul receives healing and becomes whole.

Religious traditions around the world use the labyrinth. The most famous Christian example of a labyrinth was inlaid in the floor of the cathedral at Chartres, France, during the thirteenth century. Pilgrims have come from all over the world to pray as they walk the path of this labyrinth. In the eleventh and twelfth centuries the church instructed good Christians to make at least one pilgrimage to the Holy Land in their lifetime. Because travel to the Holy Land was very expensive and dangerous, labyrinths were laid out in six different cathedrals in Europe so that people could make a symbolic pilgrimage. Over time, walking the labyrinth became a symbol for the spiritual journey and an aid to meditation, which included traditional prayers for both physical and spiritual healing and new life in the Spirit.

An international movement to encourage use of the labyrinth is now based in Grace Cathedral in San Francisco. The director of this project, Lauren Artress, describes the labyrinth as "safe territory for many who feel they are unraveling at the seams; it is a place to order chaos and calm the frightened heart."[46] For many, walking the labyrinth brings relief from stress, peace, insight, comfort, inspiration, direction, and a powerful sense of the presence of God in Christ. An individual may walk the labyrinth alone, or a group may share the walk as part of a community worship time. It is customary to remove one's shoes to walk the labyrinth.

Traditionally, walking the labyrinth is a three-step process. In the first stage, "Purgation," the walker can release whatever needs to be let go, spend time centering and quieting, become open and receptive. In the second stage, "Illumination," the walker reaches the center and spends time in receptive meditation and prayer. The third stage, experienced while walking out from the center, is "Union." The walker responds with willingness to incorporate what has been received into his or her life and to draw on the power to do that. Here are suggestions for walking the labyrinth from Scarritt-Bennett Center, a retreat center:

Guidelines for the Walk

- Clear your mind and become aware of your breath.

- Allow yourself to find the pace at which your body wants to go. You may pass people or let others step around you, whichever is easier, at the turns.

- The path goes two ways. Those going in will meet those coming out. Keep your eyes soft and your heart open.

- Do what feels natural.

E X A M P L E S

A labyrinth may be a permanent fixture or a portable cloth. A cloth as small as twenty-three feet in diameter can accommodate the pattern, although the more common size is based on the Chartres labyrinth at forty-two feet in diameter. Such a cloth may be unfolded on the floor for use and refolded for storage or transport. Priscilla Hanford writes that her congregation makes the labyrinth available year-round in connection with a Taizé service on the first Sunday evening of each month. During Lent, Taizé services are held every Sunday evening, and the labyrinth is available all day every day during Holy Week. Candlelight sets a meditative mood, and a candlelit icon sits at each corner of the canvas cloth. An icon could be a beautiful Bible, a sculpture, a painting, or any object that inspires a meditative pause on the walk. Holy Communion and "Prayers around the Cross" (during which people may approach a large wooden cross on the chancel steps and kneel, touch the cross, and pray) are added to the service in alternate months during the year. During the forty-five-minute service of music, prayer, and scripture, people are free to walk the labyrinth at any time.

V O I C E S   O F   E X P E R I E N C E

❖ Coordinate use of the labyrinth in worship with the pastor.

❖ Someone deeply committed to its values should lead in planning and organizing the use of the labyrinth.

❖ People certainly can walk the labyrinth in silence, but quiet, meditative music enriches the experience if its quality is good. A piano or guitar alone may suffice, or other instruments may be added. Recorded music can be used effectively.

❖ Allow twenty to twenty-five minutes for walking the labyrinth.

❖ Teens and older children can be involved in the labyrinth walk.

19 Prayer Walking

One of the activities scheduled for the tenth-anniversary weekend celebration at the United Methodist Church of the Resurrection was a guided prayer walk on Saturday afternoon. Printed guides were distributed prior to the walk so that families, individuals, or small groups could make a pilgrimage that recalled the history of the congregation, stopping to pray at each marker along the way. The itinerary began at the funeral home where the first services of the new church were held. This prayer suggestion was provided: "Thank God for the pioneers who took the steps of faith to start a new church. Ask God to continue to use this church as a light to the community and to bless all those who will be touched by this church in the future." The second stop was a public school that served as the next church home, and the corresponding prayer suggestion: "Praise God for [God's] promise to always be with us, whenever two or more are gathered in Jesus' name—wherever we might be gathering." At the third stop, walkers found the first building owned by the congregation. Originally a run-down, deserted sports center, it had been transformed into space for an outreach program for children and youth. The walkers read this prayer suggestion: "Ask God to help you see the potential in everything and everyone around you."

The fourth stop marked the location where groundbreaking for the present church structure had taken place, and subsequent stops were located at portions of the building in the order in which they were constructed. Prayers for the ministries in each location were suggested.

The tour concluded at a point where future building was envisioned, and the guide suggested prayers of thanksgiving for all that had been and prayers for what might yet be. Members of the congregation were posted at each stop to give additional historical background and to share in the prayers. A cassette tape with historical information and prayer suggestions was available for listening while moving between stops.

The music staff and team of this same church invited the congregation to join with them in a prayer walk through the sanctuary to lift up their special music presentation for the Lenten/Easter season. The prayers focused on petition for God to work through all parts of the program to bring alive the true message of Christ's death and resurrection. For six days prior to the presentation, the sanctuary was open during the morning hours for people to drop in at their convenience. Printed guides were available. Visitors could choose to walk around to the different locations noted in the prayer guide, to stand in the middle of the sanctuary, or sit in a pew and "walk" with their eyes and mind. A one-hour group walk was scheduled for one day, and the staff came to the sanctuary to share in the prayer after their weekly staff chapel. Prayer suggestions included the following:

> *Begin in the narthex to pray for people coming to worship, for them to be inspired and to understand the powerful message of Jesus our Savior's love and amazing grace.*

1. *Choose a place in the sanctuary to stand or to sit or to walk the rows and offer prayer for the ones who will be seated there. Pray for them to feel the presence of God in a powerful way that brings hope and a sense of the wondrous love and grace in Jesus Christ through the music and dramatic action.*

2. *Look up into the choir loft or go up the steps and sit in a choir chair. Look out into the sanctuary. Pray for the choir, soloists, dancers, narrator, and stage support people. Pray that they allow the Spirit to speak through them in words, smiles, movement, and music.*

3. *Again look out into the sanctuary and onto the stage and pray for the many children who will partner with adults and share in this time together. Pray for them to have patience and to have a meaningful experience that helps them understand Jesus' love for them.*

4. *Look into the orchestra area, sit in a chair, or stand in the conductor's place. Pray for the musicians to be strengthened for each presentation, for their melodies and harmonies to flow from their heart as they share their gift of music. Pray for the director to have strength, clear focus, and a sense of joy and peace as he directs.*

5. *Look up into the balcony at the sound/video booth or go up and sit in a chair in the balcony or stand in the booth. Pray for the technical support team to have clear focus and attention*

*to detail, to feel a sense of calm in their spirit
amidst all the demands before them.*

6. *Kneel at the altar and offer your own personal
   prayer requests and a prayer of thanksgiving
   and praise for God's wondrous love and grace
   revealed in Christ to you and to all who come to
   this church.*

Prayer walking is a ministry of intercession.
People's prayers relate to places where they
walk. Prayer walking can be a simple outing for
two friends in their own neighborhood or an
ecumenical, community-wide event. The purpose of the walk may be to pray for God's blessing on the residents of a community, on
students and teachers in a school or on a college
campus, or on workers in an office or factory.
The walk may wind through a troubled neighborhood or a place where a traumatic event has
occurred, incorporating prayers for redemption
and healing for people affected. Some walks
may prepare participants for an evangelistic
outreach or church planting effort in a new
community or for the beginning of a new service project in a neighborhood. Other walks
may include a vista point from which a whole
city or community can be seen and lift up
prayers for all included in the view. The format
is simple, the possibilities wide-ranging.

Steve Hawthorne and Graham Kendrick,
authors of a basic manual for prayer walking,
Prayerwalking: Praying On-Site with Insight,

report that though prayer walking is practiced around the world today, they have not been able to identify a single source or "authoritative, original method for the practice."[47] The popularity of prayer walking seems to have developed since the late 1970s. In early prayer walks, which were evangelistic in their intent, "Thy kingdom come in this place and to these people" was the central intercession. In the broadest sense of prayer walking, this remains the underlying prayer.

A prayer walk is not intended to attract attention to the presence of the walkers but to provide visual stimulation for prayer and insight into the realities and needs of a particular place and of people there. People typically see a place through the screen of their own personal needs and interests there. As prayer walkers they seek a new perspective, asking, "God, help me to see this place and these people through your eyes and to understand your will here." The prayers of the walkers then become open to the inspiration of the Holy Spirit and to a new awareness. As people walk and look and pray, their prayers will expand and take on new and unexpected dimensions. This experience is reflected in the phrase "praying on-site with insight" used by Hawthorne and Kendrick in the title of their book.

Prayer walking makes possible the ancient practice of touching or laying on of hands in the process of blessing. A school or office on a prayer walk may be touched as a prayer of blessing is prayed. Priscilla Van Giesen's church used the prayer walk as a way to consecrate a new education building. People who staffed the offices and classrooms were in their assigned places as prayer walkers came through. Groups visited with staff, discussed their visions and dreams for their work, and then prayed with them for their ministry in their workplace. During a process such as this, hands may be laid on workers as they permit and on parts of the building and equipment touched during prayer.

E X A M P L E

Steve Hawthorne and Graham Kendrick describe three stages of a prayer walk: preparing, praying, and reporting. In the preparation stage, before going out to walk, walkers need to orient themselves to the task ahead, to one another, and to God. At the gathering place and time, Hawthorne and Kendrick recommend three preparatory measures:

1. Refresh yourself in God. Prepare your heart with praise. Gather your mind by fixing attention on the purposes, ways, and thoughts of God and by leaving personal concerns with God. Seek God's guidance on how to pray during the walk.

2. Refresh relationships. Get to know other walkers. If there are tensions or stresses, forgive each other. And claim the presence of God with you.

3. Brief the team. Organize prayer teams; designate routes, areas, or sites; agree on timing; review topics for prayer; emphasize the significance of the walk's purpose.[48]

The second stage is the walk itself. The basic principle here is to remember that you are walking where God has long been and praying for those about whom God cares. These are the responsibilities of a prayer walker:

1. Open your eyes and look. Ask God to show you what you need to see.

2. Open your mouth and pray. Pray both silently and aloud what the Spirit directs.

3. Pray with others. Follow and reinforce the prayers offered by others on your team. The prayer of one may stimulate the prayer of another. The same prayers can be repeated and may improve with repetition. Intercession may be interrupted by conversation about what you feel, where you will go next, and what prayers should be lifted.

4. Pray with scripture. The leadership team may provide scripture resources

appropriate to the theme or purpose of the prayer walk.

5. Pray with relevance. Pray with sensitivity to the reality of the people and places you visit. Reflect on what God wants for them.

After the walk, gather the walkers to report and share significant prayers and insights. Record what was done as needed, and evaluate the experience for future planning.[49]

VOICES OF EXPERIENCE

❖ Walk in teams of two or three.

❖ Allowing at least two hours for a group prayer walk in a community ensures time for preparation and reporting as well as the walking.

❖ Prayer walking with large groups may involve extra logistical provisions. City regulations may require permits for group activities of a certain size in public areas or for the use of public address equipment. Liability insurance may be a good idea. Media contacts can be arranged if appropriate.

❖ Encourage prayer walkers to pray in positive terms, to focus on possibilities rather than problems, and to look for God's presence and activity in the situations or for the people for whom they intercede. Ask them to imagine what God's will might be for the future here and to pray for that will to be done.

20 The Prayer Place

Kathy Crane read in a magazine about a special ministry in Manhattan called a Prayer Station. When people stopped there, they received prayer for their "felt needs." That would work here, *Kathy thought.* We are on Main Street in downtown. There is a welcoming plaza outside the front doors. People pass by on the sidewalk outside our church. We could minister to the community by praying for them!

The idea grew. Members of Kathy's church constructed a tower of PVC pipes with a blue felt cover near the top carrying the words Prayer Place *in white felt letters. They made aprons of bright blue fabric with the word* Pray *and a cross in white on the front for staff to wear. Prayer Place made its debut on Super Saturday, the kick-off for the county United Way campaign. Store owners and agencies of United Way had set up tables along the street for several blocks. Kathy and her team placed the Prayer Place tower in front of the church with a table nearby offering flyers about prayer. There was no promotional material about the church; this was just an offer to pray with people. Four people from the church's prayer group donned the aprons, and during the day they prayed with an estimated two hundred people.*

Before Christmas, a community evening of "Art, Spirit, and Song" on Main Street again attracted crowds. Churches and art galleries were open, and several churches featured choirs singing Christmas music. Kathy and her team again set up Prayer Place and prayed with two hundred people who passed by in little over an hour.

Response was positive. The people who wore the aprons and offered to pray with people passing by found the experience to be "heartwarming," "meaningful," "inspiring," and "rewarding." Anne Hornkohl, a psychologist, found "a big awareness of each and every person needing the love of Christ through prayer." This outreach "brought the world close on a very personal level," she reported to Kathy. "When someone looks you in the eye and shares a very deep private concern, you are blessed to have been offered the opportunity to share in another person's life. It gave me great hope to realize that most of us who walk anonymously in the world share the same pain and joy!" Lore Baymor, a retired high-school German teacher, was surprised at how much spirituality existed in her community and at how many people were receptive to prayer. "People were not embarrassed to stand on the sidewalk in front of our church and pray for so many needs in their lives. They thanked us, but I felt that I should have thanked them." Kathy reports, "We have prayed with hundreds of people, and we have been deeply touched by the experience. I highly recommend this ministry. It meets people's needs where they are, and they seem very grateful to find people who care."

Prayer Stations is a program launched in late 1992 in New York State under the auspices of Youth With A Mission. The original purpose was evangelistic. For their annual New Year's

Eve Outreach that year, a group set up a Prayer Station on a street in Manhattan and invited people to stop and receive prayer for their felt needs. The program generated a warmly positive response.

The biblical record of the first-century church includes many examples of prayer for people in the marketplace of that time. Jesus and the apostles of the early church prayed for healing and for miracles, and the results of their prayers drew attention to the good news of the gospel. Those who prayed with people at the first New York Prayer Stations also began with life issues—job problems, family difficulties, physical needs, social needs—and found that people's hearts were opened to hear and respond to the gospel. The adaptation of the Prayer Station idea as Prayer Place in the example above was designed to express the caring ministry of a church in the community. Church members go out into the streets to make themselves available to pray with people about their concerns.

VOICES OF EXPERIENCE

Kathy Crane makes the following suggestions for leaders of a Prayer Place:

❖ Solicit the support of the pastor(s) and the church board to gain status as a ministry of the church.

❖ Train people in advance so they will be comfortable in this ministry.

❖ Include people as they are ready; some may want to observe at first.

❖ Pray as a team in advance and in the area of the planned Prayer Place before you actually begin to pray with others.

❖ Plan to offer the Prayer Place in conjunction with another event with which it fits well.

21 Concert of Prayer

Puritan minister Jonathan Edwards in the 1740s wrote a book to which he gave the title An Humble Attempt To Promote Explicit Agreement And Visible Union Of God's People In Extraordinary Prayer Of The Revival Of Religion And The Advancement Of Christ's Kingdom On Earth. *Edwards wrote the book to equip people for a prayer movement at the time in history referred to now as the First Great Awakening.*

David Bryant, who has written guidance materials for the contemporary Concerts of Prayer ministry, sees Edwards's title as a description of what the prayer concert is intended to do in our time. Bryant describes a recurring video-vision that appears on his mental terminal:

I see myself standing at the far end of a darkened hallway lined with many doors. All are shut and locked, but one. Light penetrates the hallway through a partially opened door at the far end.

. . . I walk down the hallway toward the light. The closer I get to the door, the more brilliant and delightful the light appears to be. I even begin to feel its warmth.

. . . I knock deliberately and boldly, compelled by

195

the conviction that until there is an answer I have little else to live for, as the hallway behind me promises little worth seeking.

. . . Others are quietly rising out of the shadows of the hallway to join me. We knock together now. . . . Our knocking attracts still others, until the threshold is crowded. . . .

It strikes me that when the door finally does swing open to us and we are able to move into the glorious treasures that lie beyond, the blessing will not be for us alone. The light into which we step will, at the same moment, pour beyond us to the far ends of the hallway. . . .

What does it all mean? . . . The knocking on the door is prayer. The light coming through the crack in the door is the "light of the knowledge of the glory of God in the face of Christ" (2 Cor. 4:6). The hallway represents the Church today, much of which survives in the twilight zone of all that God originally intended for us, in us, and through us. The sealed side-rooms symbolize enclaves and even whole nations, where Christ is not known.

The locked doors, waiting to be overcome by grace and truth, include structures and powers, injustices and crises, cultures and languages, persuasions old and new, that raise formidable barriers against the advancement of the Kingdom.

Those who gather at the threshold with me are members of the Lord's company—ordinary people who, already drawn to the light and benefiting from it, are hungry to know the fullness of Christ in their lives and to see the fulfillment of His purposes among the nations. The flinging wide of the central door is "spiritual awakening." . . .

The chorus of knockers represents the current development of concerted prayer for spiritual awakening.[50]

A Concert of Prayer is a gathering for prayer. The design of the order of worship for a Concert of Prayer allows time for corporate, small-group, and individual prayer—both spoken and sung. Scripture readings are included as models for prayer and as keys to the theme for a particular Concert of Prayer, but there is no sermon, and teaching is limited to interpreting a specific theme and guiding the service.

The focus in a prayer concert is on two themes: church renewal and world evangelization. David Bryant, who developed the Concerts of Prayer program out of his work with InterVarsity Christian Fellowship, uses the words *fullness* and *fulfillment* for these two themes. Prayers ask God (1) to reveal the fullness of Christ as Lord to the church, bringing revival, renewal, and awakening, and (2) for the fulfillment of God's cause through the church, including advancement of the kingdom through missions and world evangelization.[51]

The word *concert* has a double meaning here. First, it refers to the unity of those who pray "in concert" with one another. But the musical metaphor of a concert also describes the dynamics of prayer. Bryant calls a Concert of Prayer a "harmonious celebration," which is "like a grand symphony—as pray-ers blend their hearts, minds and voices by faith in God's Word. Rejoicing, repenting, and making requests, they intercede in harmony with all God has promised for [God's] Church and for [God's] world."[52]

For Bryant the two primary themes—fullness and fulfillment—are the treble and bass clefs of a musical score. The conductor is Jesus Christ, and the score is the scriptures. Believers united in prayer can release the music of God's kingdom purposes for the whole world to hear. In the format for a Concert of Prayer, people pray with partners, in "huddles" or groups of six, and in larger groups—duets, ensembles, and the full symphony.[53] The Concert of Prayer is intended to be a way for diverse groups to gather in unity—the faith community of a city or campus, for example.

E X A M P L E

In his book David Bryant provides a suggested format for a two-hour Concert of Prayer as a starting point for planning. He notes that this same order may be applied to a thirty-minute time frame simply by changing time allotments for the segments. The basic components are Celebration, Preparation, Dedication, Seeking for Fullness, Seeking for Fulfillment, Testimonies, and Grand Finale.

Celebration (15 minutes)

- Praise in hymns and choruses, focused on awakening and mission
- Reports of God's answers to prayers offered up during previous concerts
- Prayers of praise for God's faithfulness, for [God's] Kingdom, for [God's] Son

Preparation (20 minutes)

- Welcome to the concert!
- Overview: Why are we here?
- Biblical perspectives on what we're praying (toward awakening, mission)
- Preview of the format
- Teaming up in partners and in huddles

Dedication (5 minutes)

- Commitment to be servants through prayer and to be used in answer to our prayers
- Thanksgiving for the privilege of united prayer and for those with whom we unite
- Invitation to Christ to lead the concert and to pray through us
- Hymn of praise

199

Seeking for Fullness/Awakening in the Church (30 minutes)

- In partners—for personal revival
- In huddles—for awakening in our local churches and ministries
- As a whole—for awakening in the Church worldwide
- Pause to listen to our Father
- Chorus

Seeking for Fulfillment/Mission among the Nations (30 minutes)

- In partners—for personal ministries
- In huddles—for outreach and mission in our city or campus
- As a whole—for world evangelization
- Pause to listen to our Father
- Chorus

Testimonies: What Has God Said to Us Here? (10 minutes)

- On fullness (awakening)
- On fulfillment (mission)

Grand Finale (10 minutes)

- Offering ourselves to be answers to our prayers and also to live accordingly

- Prayer for God's empowerment in our own lives for ministry
- Prayer for prayer movements locally and worldwide
- Offering praise to the Father who will answer our Concert of Prayer.
- Leave to watch and serve "in concert"[54]

VOICES OF EXPERIENCE

❖ Participants appreciate guidance on how to participate in the Concert of Prayer—how long individual prayers may be, when to speak, and when to be quiet.

❖ Emphasis on tolerance for a diversity of prayer styles enables a Concert of Prayer to reach across divisions in the Christian community.

❖ The format presented above could be used in a regular service of worship or on a special occasion, such as Pentecost Sunday.

❖ The Concert of Prayer as a one-time or occasional event provides a good opportunity for gathering several churches together to pray about shared local concerns and common visions of the kingdom.

❖ A printed program and set of guidelines will help participants to understand and follow the format's flow.

❖ The Concert of Prayer format works either for a small group in an average-sized room or a large group in an auditorium.

22 *Prayer Classes*

> Helping another person learn to pray is an
> awesome opportunity. Prayer comes naturally
> to us, but at the same time, prayer is a skill that
> can be learned (and taught). It is a dimension of
> our faith journey that can grow across the
> years. We can help each other grow in prayer.[55]

Teaching people how to pray is the key to a
strong prayer ministry in any church. Study
groups, classes, workshops, seminars, retreats,
or other training programs designed to help
people learn how to pray constitute an excellent
launch for a new prayer ministry. And as a congregation takes steps toward a richer prayer
life, adding new formats, training will make the
difference in the long-term health of the expansion. Since new people will come into the congregation with an interest in the spiritual
discipline of prayer, maintaining ongoing programs of prayer instruction is important.

Congregations also may schedule prayer
classes in response to expressed needs and

questions about prayer. A person invited to be part of a prayer chain, to participate in a prayer vigil, or to be a prayer partner may respond with feelings of inadequacy and questions about what to pray and how and why. A prayer class can provide resources for working on both the theology and the practice of prayer. Such educational opportunities may take on an almost infinite variety of forms. The most popular setting is the short-term study group with five to twelve sessions. Established groups, such as Sunday-school classes, women's groups, or youth groups, may designate prayer as the study theme for a period of time. Retreats, summer camps for youth, vacation Bible schools, youth assemblies, adult camps, and adult assemblies all offer opportunities for people to learn to pray. Basic principles about how to pray can be taught in a one-time event.

Prayer groups themselves often include an educational dimension, devoting a portion of their time together to study and reflection on prayer. Individuals may benefit from one-on-one tutoring with a spiritual director, spiritual friend, or spiritual companion.

E X A M P L E S

A wealth of resources—books, videotapes, denominational and independent Christian organizations, and Web sites—is available for leaders and independent learners. Here are some sources.

Book-based prayer studies. Upper Room Books, publisher of this book, has provided books for prayer studies for many years. Several titles now offer accompanying videotapes, and a number are written in workbook form, providing study group members guidance for individual reading, reflecting, and praying between meetings. Some of the most popular of these books currently available are:

- *The Workbook of Living Prayer* by Maxie Dunnam. This workbook teaches how to pray in a simple, practical way. Widely appreciated as an introductory resource, the six-week format includes daily Bible readings and prayer exercises combined with suggestions for weekly group meetings. An accompanying video provides a ten-minute message for each week.

- *Responding to God: A Guide to Daily Prayer* and *Responding to God: Leader's Guide* by Martha Graybeal Rowlett. The basic text deals with both the theology of prayer and the practice of prayer. Three questions are addressed: "How can I think about prayer?" "How can I pray?" and "What difference does prayer make?" Questions about the nature of God and prayer open the study, and traditional forms of prayer are described: meditation, praise and adoration, confession, petition, intercession, and thanksgiving. Each chapter includes a "Guide for Daily Prayer."

The Leader's Guide offers guidance for leading six-week, ten-week, twelve-week, or retreat studies of the text. The appendix includes expanded materials on intercessory prayer and unanswered prayer and provides two extra guides to daily prayer that deal specifically with these topics.

- *The Workbook of Intercessory Prayer* by Maxie Dunnam. A seven-week study giving special attention to prayer for others. Session topics include (1) Getting Intercession into Perspective, (2) Immersing Ourselves in Scripture, (3) Overcoming Some Hurdles, (4) Some Essential Principles of Intercession, (5) Keys for Effective Intercession, (6) Using Imagination and Practicing Nonverbal Prayer, and (7) The Intercessor.

- *The Breath of Life: A Workbook* by Ron Del-Bene with Mary and Herb Montgomery. This five-session group study encourages pray-ers to be in continuous communication with God through a breath prayer—a simple phrase that expresses what is always in our hearts. A related video, *Learning the Breath Prayer,* is available.

- *Alone with God: A Workbook* by Ron Del-Bene with Mary and Herb Montgomery. This workbook offers six weekly group sessions and individual daily activities for thirty days to increase attentiveness to God's presence. The *Praying the Scriptures* video is recommended with this study.

- *Devotional Life in the Wesleyan Tradition: A Workbook* by Steve Harper. This seven-week study explores major features in John Wesley's devotional life.

Web-based prayer course. Spirituality: Invitation to a Closer Relationship with God is an eight-session online course offered by the Evangelical Lutheran Church in America. The class is a virtual community of people who take the course together. An online bulletin board enables conversation among course participants and the authors. Class members sign up by purchasing a participant's book and audio packet that contains comments by the authors, meditation activities and music. A congregational packet provides leader helps; background information; class handouts; time schedules for sixty- or ninety-minute sessions; videotaped presentations by Richard Foster, Thomas Moore,

Frederick Buechner, Marjory Zoet Bankson, Joseph Sittler, and Garrison Keillor; promotional material; and information about the Spirituality WebBoard with ID number for access to online conferencing. These resources are available from Augsburg Press at 1-800-328-4648.

Church-based seminar. Priscilla Van Giesen's large church offered a two-hour session entitled Prayer and Praise Event for Children, Youth, and Adults. The theme was Prayer Alive! This model and format could be adapted for use in any church.

The publicity for Prayer Alive! outlined the event: "After gathering for fellowship and snacks, we will share together from 7–7:30 P.M. in an uplifting and inspiring time of music, singing, and prayer. . . . This will be followed by 9 choices for learning about prayer from 7:45 to 8:30 P.M." The choices included the following:

- Prayer in a Bottle: Children and Parents Together
- ACTS Prayer Taster for Youth
- Prayer 101—Prayer Basics: Where Do We Begin?
- Conversational Prayer: Building a Relationship with God
- Take Time to Be Holy: A Place and Space for Prayer in Your Life

- Praying the Scriptures: *Lectio Divina*, the Divine Word
- Health and Wholeness: What a Difference Prayer Makes
- The Power of Intercessory Prayer
- Prayer of Cleansing and Renewal: The Heart and Soul of Daily Life

VOICES OF EXPERIENCE

❖ The leader for a study on prayer does not have to be an expert on prayer. The Holy Spirit is the ultimate teacher. A good leader simply is growing in the life of prayer and is willing to share the pilgrimage with others who want to grow.

❖ People learn best by doing. The more actively involved in the learning process a person becomes, the more effective the learning is. Learning to pray happens when people actually pray—in a group and in the time between group meetings.

❖ The environment for learning is important. For prayer classes, secure a comfortable and quiet space free from interruptions and distractions.

❖ The learning experience for each person must begin where he or she is. Some persons have little or no experience with prayer. Others have had unpleasant or unproductive experiences that they have to overcome before they can learn new, positive ways of praying. Some may have had a rich and meaningful prayer life out of which to share with the group. Each person needs to feel comfortable in beginning at his or her own place and growing from that point.

❖ One of the joys of teaching adults is that adults tend to come to groups highly motivated to learn. The leader collaborates with them in a common endeavor.[56]

Concluding Observations

Only a few churches tell their stories here. These stories are the tip of the iceberg. For every church represented, there are thousands more where Christians carry on the tradition of our faith and pray together. All have unique stories to tell, but some common themes appear. In summary I offer a few general conclusions drawn from the research for this project.

The scientific and technological revolutions of the last two centuries have not shaken the church's faith in the power of prayer. Contributors have been enthusiastic about their experiences of praying together with others. They are eager to share the important, transforming, valuable things happening to them and to other people. They have stories to tell and a witness to make to the power of the Spirit in their midst and in the world.

The contributors are excited not about the structures they describe but about what happens inside those structures. Many contributors acknowledge that a prayer chain, a prayer group, or a prayer class was the doorway through which they walked into a new relationship with God. They are grateful for that experience and want other people to have access to doorways too. For this reason, they happily talk about the details of "doors"—the structures that encourage authentic community prayer.

Contemporary Christians are figuring out ways to pray together. This book is the third in a series on prayer developed for use in the local church. The first two books (*Responding to God: A Guide to Daily Prayer* and *Responding to God: Leader's Guide)* focus primarily on an individual's experience of prayer. Prayer is defined as "openness" to the presence of God and to communion between God's spirit and a person's human spirit. Sometimes that openness takes the form of *listening* to God. Sometimes we pray by *talking* to God. Prayer can be adoration and praise and meditation and contemplation—experiences of openness *to* God. Prayer can also be thanksgiving, intercession, and petition—openness *with* God. This book reports that prayer in all of its dimensions as individual experience makes up part of our community experience as well. We gather to sit in silent contemplation together. We pray the scriptures together, listening to hear God's Word for us. We link up with others to intercede together as a way to bear one another's burdens. We meet to support one another in developing the holy habit of regular prayer. If we can pray by ourselves, we can pray together.

The creative ways in which people have organized themselves to pray together are significant. A few basic patterns seem to be widely known and used. But local congregations create their unique ways of using these patterns, adapting to local circumstances and the personalities and life situations of those involved. Other patterns of community prayer are less well known, but where they are used, again people demonstrate remarkably creative adaptations. If the Spirit moves among people who gather to pray, the form of their meeting is not frozen in a set pattern but continually is recreated and made new. One group's experience becomes another group's launching pad.

At the same time, contributors offer warnings and report what can go wrong or cause problems when gathering to pray together. They agree that attention to the health of a group and to the details of the process is important. Some things work and some things don't. It does not pay to be careless or naive.

Children and youth frequently participate in praying together, according to the research. Young people can use almost all the models described here, either in youth ministries or in intergenerational settings. Some of the most innovative models here began as youth ministries and later were adopted by adults. Children are quite capable of praying with one another and with adults. Even nursery school–age children regularly share with others in prayer as they have grace at snack time in their classes or during devotional time in their homes with their families. Intergenerational sharing in prayer can be good for all ages as different perspectives are shared.

Finally, when the experience of praying is alive for people in a congregation, prayer ministries will emerge. People figure out ways to share their experience with others. The key factor in the development of prayer ministries in local churches is obviously not the size or budget or location of the church. Prayer ministries thrive where people already are responding to the initiative of the Holy Spirit and are experiencing the transformational power of prayer.

Resources

Prayer in Congregational Worship
Denominational worship books
Duck, Ruth C. *Finding Words for Worship: A Guide for Leaders.* Louisville, Ky.: Westminster John Knox Press, 1995.

Huffman, Walter C. *The Prayer of the Faithful: Understanding and Creatively Leading Corporate Intercessory Prayer.* Minneapolis, Minn.: Augsburg Fortress Publishers, 1992.

Stookey, Laurence Hull. *Let the Whole Church Say Amen!* Nashville, Tenn.: Abingdon Press, 2001.

The Taizé Community makes available songbooks and recorded music in several languages. These materials are copyrighted but available for local use with permission. Information on these resources and other helpful tips on planning and leading Taizé prayer can be found on their Web site: www.taize.fr.

Intercessory Prayer
Dunnam, Maxie. *The Workbook of Intercessory Prayer.* Nashville, Tenn.: The Upper Room, 1979.

Pray! magazine 12 (May/June 1999) and 22 (January/February 2001). To order: Contact The Navigators, P.O. Box 35004, Colorado Springs, CO 80935-3504. 1-800-366-7788.

Prayer Station Kits with manual and video are available from Youth With A Mission, 70 New York Ave., Smithtown, NY 11787. 1-631-366-1000. info@ywam-ny.com.

Teykl, Terry. *Making a Room to Pray.* Muncie, Indiana: Prayer Point Press, 1993. For suggestions on selecting and training volunteers for telephone prayer ministries see Chapter 7: Planning a Telephone Prayer Ministry.

The Upper Room Living Prayer Center. 1908 Grand Avenue, P.O. Box 340004, Nashville, Tennessee 37203-0004. Toll free: 1-877-899-2780 ext. 7215. www.upperroom.org. Prayer Request line: 1-800-251-2468.

Vennard, Jane E. *Praying for Friends and Enemies: Intercessory Prayer.* Minneapolis, Minn.: Augsburg Fortress, 1995.

Prayers for Healing

Benedict, Dan. "Healing Ministry and Worship." Article on the GBOD Web site: http://www.gbod.org/worship/articles/healing.html.

Denominational Books of Worship

Penn, John. "What Everyone Should Know about Healing." Available from the author at P.O. Box 1344, Antioch, TN 37011-1344.

Wagner, James K. *An Adventure in Healing and Wholeness*. Nashville, Tenn.: Upper Room Books, 1993.

Prayer Retreats

Job, Rueben P. *Spiritual Life in the Congregation: A Guide for Retreats*. Nashville, Tenn.: Upper Room Books, 1997.

Rowlett, Martha Graybeal. *Responding to God: Leader's Guide*. Nashville, Tenn.: Upper Room Books, 2000.

Shawchuck, Norman, Rueben P. Job, and Robert G. Doherty. *How to Conduct a Spiritual Life Retreat*. Nashville, Tenn.: The Upper Room, 1986.

Praying the Scriptures

Bohler, Carolyn Stahl. *Opening to God: Guided Imagery Meditation on Scripture*. Nashville, Tenn.: Upper Room Books, 1996.

Mulholland, M. Robert, Jr. *Shaped by the Word*. Nashville, Tenn.: Upper Room Books, 2000.

Spiritual Formation Bible: *Growing in Intimacy with God through Scripture*. New Revised Standard Version. Grand Rapids, Mich.: Zondervan Publishing House, 1999.

Vest, Norvene. *Gathered in the Word: Praying the Scripture in Small Groups*. Nashville, Tenn.: Upper Room Books, 1996.

Centering Prayer

Keating, Thomas. O*pen Mind, Open Heart: The Contemplative Dimension of the Gospel.* New York: Continuum International Publishing Group, 1994.

―――. *The Method of Centering Prayer.* Butler, N.J.: Contemplative Outreach, 1995.

―――. Videotape sets on the practice of contemplative prayer. Contemplative Outreach, Ltd. 10 Park Place, Suite 2B, P.O. Box 737, Butler, New Jersey 07405. Phone: 973-838-3384. www.contemplativeoutreach.org.

Prayer in Planning and Decision Making

Morris, Danny E. *Yearning to Know God's Will: A Workbook for Discerning God's Guidance for Your Life.* Grand Rapids, Mich.: Zondervan, 1991.

Morris, Danny E., and Charles M. Olsen. *Discerning God's Will Together: A Spiritual Practice for the Church.* Nashville, Tenn.: Upper Room Books, 1997.

Olsen, Charles M. *Transforming Church Boards into Communities of Spiritual Leaders.* Bethesda, Md.: The Alban Institute, 1995.

Stevens, Garrie, Pamela Lardear, and Sharon Duger. *Seeking and Doing God's Will: Discernment for the Community of Faith.* Nashville, Tenn.: Discipleship Resources, 1998.

Worshipful-Work. 17000 NW 45 Hwy., Kansas City, Missouri 64152; e-mail WorshpfulW@ aol.com. http://www.worshipful-work.org

Family Prayer

For ordering information:

The Upper Room Web site: www.upperroom.org.

To order *The Upper Room* daily devotional guide, *Devo'Zine*, and *Pockets*, call 1-800-925-6847 or go online at The Upper Room Web site.

Cloyd, Betty Shannon. *Children and Prayer: A Shared Pilgrimage.* Nashville, Tenn.: Upper Room Books, 1997.

———. *Parents and Grandparents as Spiritual Guides: Nurturing Children of the Promise.* Nashville, Tenn.: Upper Room Books, 2000.

Downing, Sue. *Hand in Hand: Growing Spiritually with Our Children.* Nashville, Tenn.: Discipleship Resources, 1998.

Halverson, Delia Touchton. *How Do Our Children Grow? Introducing Children to God, Jesus, the Bible, Prayer, Church.* St. Louis, Mo.: Chalice Press, 1999.

Isbell, Rick and Sue Isbell. *Capture the Moment: Building Faith Traditions for Families.* Nashville, Tenn.: Discipleship Resources, 1998.

Park, Andrew Sungho, Brandon Cho, Kyungsig Samuel Lee, and Heisik Oh. *Korean Family Devotions.* Nashville, Tenn.: Upper Room Books, 1994.

Payden, Deborah A., and Laura Loving. *Celebrating at Home: Prayers and Liturgies for Families.* Cleveland, Ohio: Pilgrim Press, 1998.

Thompson, Marjorie J. *Family the Forming Center: A Vision of the Role of Family in Spiritual Formation.* Nashville, Tenn.: Upper Room Books, 1996.

Covenant Groups

Covenant Discipleship resources (published by and available from Discipleship Resources, 1908 Grand Avenue, Nashville, Tennessee 37212. Call 1-800-685-4370 or check online at www.discipleshipresources.org):

Harris, Edie G. and Shirley L. Ramsey. *Sprouts: Nurturing Children through Covenant Discipleship.* This guide outlines a program for children (grades 3–6) to meet weekly and support one another in their efforts to live as disciples of Christ by doing acts that demonstrate their love for God and others.

Manskar, Steven. *Accountable Discipleship: Living in God's Household* (2000). This is the foundation document that provides the theological, biblical, and historical bases for Covenant Discipleship Groups and class leaders.

Sutherland, David. *Together in Love: Covenant Discipleship with Youth.* This resource is designed to hold youth and college students accountable to one another and to Christ in a covenant that includes acts of devotion, worship, compassion, and justice.

Watson, Gayle. *Guide for Covenant Discipleship Groups* (2000). This is the basic resource for Covenant Discipleship group members.

RENOVARÉ resources:

Foster, Richard J. *Celebration of Discipline: The Path to Spiritual Growth.* Rev. ed. San Francisco: Harper & Row, 1988.
———. *Streams of Living Water: Celebrating the Great Traditions of Christian Faith.* San Francisco: HarperSanFrancisco, 1998. For more information, see www.renovare.org or write to 8 Inverness Drive East, Suite 102, Englewood, CO 80112-5624.
Smith, James Bryan, with Lynda L. Graybeal. *A Spiritual Formation Workbook: Small-Group Resources for Nurturing Christian Growth.* Rev. ed. With a foreword by Richard J. Foster. San Francisco: HarperSanFrancisco, 1993.

Prayer Room or Chapel

Prayer Point Press Staff. *Prayer Room Intercessor's Handbook.* Muncie, Ind.: Prayer Point Press, 1999.
Teykl, Terry. *Making Room to Pray.* Muncie, Ind.: Prayer Point Press, 1993.

Labyrinth

Artress, Lauren. *Walking a Sacred Path: Rediscovering the Labyrinth as a Sacred Tool.* New York:

Riverhead Books, 1995. The Web site www.gracecathedral.org gives information about the labyrinth project headquartered at Grace Cathedral in San Francisco. The online gift shop offers a Seed Kit with resources for creating a labyrinth to fit the space available.

Prayer Walking
Hawthorne, Steve, and Graham Kendrick. *Prayerwalking: Praying On-Site with Insight.* Lake Mary, Fla.: Creation House, 1993.

Concert of Prayer
Bryant, David. *How Christians Can Join Together in Concerts of Prayer for Spiritual Awakening and World Evangelization.* Ventura, Calif.: Regal Books, 1988.

Prayer Classes
See resources listed on pages 205–8 in Prayer Classes.

To request prayers from The Upper Room Living Prayer Center, call 1-800-251-2468.

To establish a Remote Prayer Center, call 1-877-899-2780 ext. 7214 or visit The Upper Room Living Prayer Center online at www.upperroom.org/prayer.

Notes

1. Kennon L. Callahan, *Twelve Keys to an Effective Church: Strategic Planning for Mission* (San Francisco: Harper and Row, 1983), xvi.
2. Ibid., xvi–xvii.
3. *The Book of Order 1998–99*, part 2 of *The Constitution of the Presbyterian Church (USA)*, (Louisville, Ky.: The Office of the General Assembly, 1998), W-2.1000.
4. *The United Methodist Book of Worship* (Nashville, Tenn.: The United Methodist Publishing House, 1992), 15.
5. *The Book of Order*, Presbyterian Church (USA), W-3.3202.
6. *The United Methodist Book of Worship*, 14.
7. Ibid., 16–32.
8. Adapted from information on Web site: www.taize.fr.
9. Harry Emerson Fosdick, *A Book of Public Prayers* (New York: Harper and Brothers, 1959), 7–8.
10. Ruth C. Duck, *Finding Words for Worship: A Guide for Leaders* (Louisville, Ky.: Westminster John Knox Press, 1995), 20, 24, 26, 25, 20, 21.
11. Martha Graybeal Rowlett, *Responding to God: A Guide to Daily Prayer* (Nashville, Tenn.: Upper Room Books, 2000), 74.
12. *The United Methodist Book of Worship*, 613–14.
13. Reginald Mallett, from a sermon preached at Lake Junaluska, N.C., July 27, 1988, quoted in James K. Wagner, *An Adventure in Healing and Wholeness* (Nashville, Tenn.: Upper Room Books, 1993), 57.
14. Wagner, *An Adventure in Healing and Wholeness*, 139–40.
15. Ibid., 140–41.

16. *The Book of Order*, Presbyterian Church (USA), W-3.5405.

17. Terry Teykl, *Making Room to Pray* (Muncie, Ind.: Prayer Point Press, 1993), 104.

18. Ibid., 105–7.

19. See www.sacredspace.ie or www.jesuit.ie/prayer/

20. Rueben P. Job, *Spiritual Life in the Congregation: A Guide for Retreats* (Nashville, Tenn.: Upper Room Books, 1997), 71–76.

21. Norvene Vest, *Gathered in the Word: Praying the Scriptures in Small Groups* (Nashville, Tenn.: Upper Room Books, 1996), 11.

22. Ibid., 17–18.

23. Adapted from Vest, *Gathered in the Word*, 18, 60–65.

24. Thomas Keating, *The Method of Centering Prayer* (Butler, N.J.: Contemplative Outreach, Ltd., 1995), brochure.

25. Ibid.

26. Garrie Stevens, Pamela Lardear, and Sharon Duger, *Seeking and Doing God's Will: Discernment for the Community of Faith* (Nashville, Tenn.: Discipleship Resources, 1998), 13.

27. From notes taken by the author at Worshipful-Work Conference, Los Angeles, California, May 1999.

28. Charles M. Olsen, *Transforming Church Boards into Communities of Spiritual Leaders* (Bethesda, Md.: The Alban Institute, 1995), 20–22.

29. Danny E. Morris and Charles M. Olsen, *Discerning God's Will Together: A Spiritual Practice for the Church* (Nashville, Tenn.: Upper Room Books, 1997/2002 printing), 85.

30. Ibid., chapter 4.

31. Olsen, *Transforming Church Boards*, 91.

32. Stevens, Lardear, and Duger, *Seeking and Doing God's Will*, 27.

33. Ibid., 29.

34. Ibid., 50.

35. Marjorie J. Thompson, *Family the Forming Center: A Vision of the Role of Family in Spiritual Formation* (Nashville, Tenn.: Upper Room Books, 1996), 90.

36. David Lowes Watson, *Forming Christian Disciples: The Role of Covenant Discipleship and Class Leaders in the Congregation* (Nashville, Tenn.: Discipleship Resources, 1995), 65.

37. Ibid., 7–8.

38. Ibid., 9.

39. Watson, *Covenant Discipleship: Christian Formation through Mutual Accountability* (Nashville, Tenn.: Discipleship Resources, 1996), 115.

40. Ibid., 150.

41. James Bryan Smith with Lynda L. Graybeal, A *Spiritual Formation Workbook*: *Small-Group Resources for Nurturing Christian Growth,* rev. ed. with a foreword by Richard J. Foster (San Francisco: HarperSanFrancisco, 1993), 9.

42. Ibid., 99.

43. Ibid., 100.

44. Ibid., 9.

45. Terry Teykl, *Making Room to Pray*, 78–79.

46. Lauren Artress, *Walking a Sacred Path: Rediscovering the Labyrinth as a Spiritual Tool* (New York: Riverhead Books, 1995), 165.

47. Steve Hawthorne and Graham Kendrick, *Prayerwalking: Praying On-Site with Insight* (Lake Mary, Fla.: Creation House, 1993), 15.

48. Ibid., 26–31.

49. Ibid., 31–33.

50. David Bryant, *How Christians Can Join Together in Concerts of Prayer for Spiritual Awakening and World Evangelization* (Ventura, Calif.: Regal Books, 1988), 18–20.

51. Ibid., 14.

52. Ibid.

53. Ibid.

54. Ibid., 101–3.

55. Martha Graybeal Rowlett, *Responding to God: Leader's Guide* (Nashville, Tenn.: Upper Room Books, 2000), 7.

56. Ibid., adapted from pages 7–11.

About the Author

MARTHA GRAYBEAL ROWLETT is a retired pastor in the California-Pacific Annual Conference of The United Methodist Church. She has served pastorates in California and Washington as well as working at the annual conference level in the California-Nevada and California-Pacific annual conferences. Dr. Rowlett received a Master's degree in Christian Education from Emory University, a Master of Divinity degree from Pacific School of Religion, and a Doctor of Ministry degree from Claremont School of Theology. Her previously published books include *Responding to God: A Guide to Daily Prayer* and the *Leader's Guide* to *Responding to God*, both published by Upper Room Books.

Other Titles of Interest from Upper Room Books

At Home with God:
Family Devotions for the School Year
by Anne Broyles, Sue Downing, Paul and
Elizabeth Lind Escamilla, Marilyn Brown Oden

Beginning Prayer
by John Killinger

A Book of Personal Prayer
compiled by René Bideaux

Children and Prayer: A Shared Pilgrimage
by Betty Shannon Cloyd

Dimensions of Prayer:
Cultivating a Relationship with God
by Douglas V. Steere

Discerning God's Will Together: A Spiritual
Practice for the Church
by Danny E. Morris and Charles M. Olsen

Family the Forming Center: A Vision of the Role of
Family in Spiritual Formation
by Marjorie J. Thompson

Fire in the Soul: A Prayer Book for the Later Years
by Richard L. Morgan

Responding to God: A Guide to Daily Prayer
by Martha Graybeal Rowlett

Responding to God: Leader's Guide
by Martha Graybeal Rowlett

Sacred Journeys: A Woman's Book of Daily Prayer
by Jan L. Richardson

Teach Me to Pray
by W. E. Sangster

*With Heart and Mind and Soul: A Guide to Prayer
for College Students and Young Adults*
by Helen R. Neinast and Thomas C. Ettinger

The Workbook of Intercessory Prayer
by Maxie Dunnam

The Workbook of Living Prayer
by Maxie Dunnam

Order online at
www.upperroom.org/bookstore

Order by phone at
1-800-972-0433

Or visit your local bookstore